D1164869

THE GREAT
WARPLANES
OF THE 1990s

THE GREAT
WARPLANES
OF THE 1990s

BILL YENNE

GALLERY BOOKS
An imprint of W.H. Smith Publishers Inc.
112 Madison Avenue
New York, New York 10016

Published by Gallery Books

A Division of W H Smith Publishers Inc
112 Madison Avenue
New York, New York 10016

Produced by
Bison Books Ltd
Kimbolton House
117A Fulham Road
London SW3 6RL

ISBN 0-8317-4075-2

Printed in Hong Kong

1 2 3 4 5 6 7 8 9 10

Page 1: McDonnell Douglas F-15A Eagles of the US Air
Force Alaskan Air Command (AAC) over Mount McKinley.
Equipped with long-range fuel tanks and live AIM-9 Side-
winder and AIM-7 Sparrow air-to-air missiles, AAC
Eagles patrol America's most rugged frontier. In recent
years, they have averaged one encounter weekly with
Soviet bombers testing them by flying within a few miles
of American territory.

Pages 2-3: A remarkable late afternoon photo of a Soviet
Air Force Sukhoi Su-27 (NATO code name Flanker) interceptor touching down with its fuselage speed brake
deployed behind the canopy. This Flanker is the Su-27U
(*Uti*) two-seat training version of the Soviet Union's foremost contemporary aircraft. For today's mission, the
pilot flies alone, although an advanced student transi-
tioning from another type of aircraft typically rides in the
rear seat.

Below: A US Air Force General Dynamics F-16 Falcon. A
single-engine fighter, the F-16 was originally procured as
a low cost complement to the F-15 Eagle. Both aircraft
are now being equipped with new Low Altitude Navigation and Targeting Infrared for Night (LANTIRN) pods to
permit low altitude operations at night or in almost any
weather.

ACKNOWLEDGEMENTS

The author wishes to thank the following people
for helping to supply material to make this book
possible: Bob Foster at McDonnell Douglas; John
Godden at British Aerospace; aviation photographer
George Hall; Robert Harwood of Grumman Aero-
space; Christina Rahm at Saab-Scania; aviation
photographer Erik Simonsen; HM Suisse at Dassault
Breguet Aviation; Joe Thornton and Joe Stout at
General Dynamics; and Major Carl von Heine, Air
Attaché Swedish Embassy.

Designed by Bill Yenne
Edited by Deirdre Levenson and Joan Hayes

PICTURE CREDITS

Australian Department of Defence 88 (center), 90
(top), 92 (bottom)
Michael Badrocke 28 (center), 106-107
British Aerospace Aircraft Group 11, 14-15, 15 (top
right silhouette), 16 (both), 17 (both), 18, 18-19,
19, 20-21, 22 (bottom), 23 (all), 24 (all), 25 (all),
58 (top), 60 (top), 61 (top right), 65, 66-67, 67
Jahn Charleville, Swedish Air Force via *Aviation
Week & Space Technology* 81 (top)
Dassault-Breguet 94-95 (all), 96 (all), 97, 98-99
(all), 100-101 (all)
General Dynamics Corporation 4-5, 9 (bottom), 12,
68, 69 (top right), 70, 72, 73 (bottom), 74 (bottom), 75, 76, 77
Claude Gluntz/RenPhot 39
Grumman 26-27, 27 (top right silhouette), 30 (top),
30-31, 32 (bottom), 33 (top), 34-35, 35
George Hall 51 (bottom left), 110-111
Ulf Hugo, Swedish Air Force via *Aviation Week &
Space Technology* 42, 81 (bottom)
McDonnell Douglas Corporation 1, 14, 21 (top right,
second from top), 46-47, 47 (top right silhouette), 48 (bottom left and right), 49, 50 (top),
50-51, 51 (bottom right), 52 (second from top),
53, 54 (top), 55 (both), 86-87, 87 (top and bottom), 89, 90 (bottom left), 90-91, 92 (top and
center), 92-93

Messerschmitt-Bölkow-Blohm 56 (bottom left),
56-57, 58 (bottom), 59 (both), 60 (bottom),
60-61, 61 (bottom), 62 (top), 63 (right), 64 (both)
Northrop 6, 109, 110, 111, 110-111
Panavia Aircraft GmbH 57 (top right), 62 (bottom
left), 63 (bottom left)
Pilot Press 28 (top and bottom)
Rockwell International 102-103, 103 (top right sil-
houette), 108, 109
SAAB Scania 78-79, 79 (top right), 80 (both), 82-83
(all), 84-85
Mickey W Sanborn, US Air Force 102 (left)
Erik Simonsen 2-3, 13, 36-37, 38 (bottom), 40-41,
42 (top), 43, 44-45, 71
Swedish Air Force via *Aviation Week & Space Tech-
nology* 8 (top left, right)

US Air Force 8 (bottom), 9 (top), 10 (all), 48 (top), 52
(top left, right), 54 (bottom), 68-69, 73, 76 (bottom), 86, 104 (top left, center), 104-105, 105,
107, 108
US Department of Defense 7, 38 (top), 42 (bottom)
US Marine Corps 22 (top)
US Navy 26, 29 (bottom), 32 (top), 33 (bottom), 74
© Bill Yenne (insignias top right of following pages)
15, 27, 37 (insignias and silhouette), 41 (insignias
and silhouette) 47, 57, 69, 79, 87, 95, 103, 41
(top left and right)

CONTENTS

INTRODUCTION

Combat aircraft, like any evolving 'species' of technology, tend to occur in generations. The generation that came of age in the 1960s were in their prime in the 1970s, even as a new generation was being flight tested. The generation that *came of age* in the 1980s, which were reviewed in the first edition of this book in 1986, are the generation that will *be* the warplanes of the 1990s and will define the nature of air power for the balance of the twentieth century.

In order to consider the warplanes of any generation, it is essential to consider combat aircraft in terms of their missions, which classically fall into two categories: tactical and strategic. Tactical air combat missions are those which have an immediate connection to a battlefield activity, while strategic missions are flown against distant targets within enemy territory for the purpose of destroying factories, airfields, railroads and materiel bound for the battlefield. While tactical missions are flown against an immediate enemy threat, strategic missions are flown against the enemy's will to fight. The theory of strategic warfare holds that if the enemy's will to fight is eradicated, there will be no battlefield.

As a rule, bombers fly strategic missions, while fighters and attack aircraft fly tactical missions. Every such rule has exceptions. Bombers have often been used on tactical missions, while fighters used to escort bombers on strategic bombing missions can be considered as strategic aircraft. In addition, aircraft specifically designed for the short-range attack role may be used on long-range or strategic missions if no bombers are available.

The division between tactical and strategic airpower is, however, tenuous. As borne out in actual practice in World War II, Korea, Vietnam and the Middle East, airpower is applied where it is needed and by those aircraft that can do the specific job at hand. Certain airmen have always bristled at the thought of pigeon-

The Northrop B-2 stealth bomber *(above)* represents the superpower distrust that persists despite the rare cooperation seen *at right*, as USAF F-15s and Canadian CF-18s escort Soviet MiG-29s to the 1989 Abottsford Air Show.

holing their airpower. As US Air Force Chief of Staff, General Hoyt Vandenberg said in 1951: 'Airpower is indivisible. We don't speak of a "strategic" or a "tactical" Army or Navy, yet those terms are constantly applied to the Air Force. The overriding purpose of every plane, whether it is a bomber or a fighter, is to win the air battle on which victory on land or sea is predicated.'

Vandenberg's viewpoint is echoed by US Air Force long range planners of the 1990s, who envision and plan for both the B-1 and B-2 strategic bombers to be able to apply their considerable firepower, and the latter's stealthy 'bag of tricks' to potential tactical targets. This sort of versatility has been designed into all of the American warplanes to come of the drawing boards since Vietnam, and is clearly evident in this book.

There is also a certain economy of scale in using one's heavy bombers for non-nuclear strike missions. For example, Operation El Dorado Canyon, the April 1986 strike on Libya, involved 120 tactical and support aircraft. US Air Force Chief of Staff Larry Welch points out that had they been available, the same goals could

have been accomplished with five B-2s flying from the United States with the help of five tankers.

It is certainly true that 'strategic' B-29s and B-52s were used in a tactical role in Korea and Vietnam, and that the 1981 raid by 'tactical' F-16s against Osirik was clearly a strategic mission. In fact, the lightweight F-16 fighter can carry a bigger bomb load than a World War II heavy bomber. Indeed, in the 1990s, as so few forces *have* dedicated 'strategic' aircraft, the delineation is applicable only to missions. Nevertheless, we will use the tactical and strategic definitions as points of reference, while realizing that there are indeed exceptions to every rule.

THE EVOLUTION OF THE BOMBER

Basically, a bomber is defined as a multiengined combat aircraft designed to carry a large bomb load over long distances. As such, they first appeared during World War I in the arsenals of Britain, Germany and Tsarist Russia. By World War II, both the bomber and the concept of strategic air power had evolved into complex and potent weapons. The strategic bombing campaign carried out by the United States and Britain against Germany and by the United States against Japan were major craft

factors in the defeat of the Axis, a fact which is clearly borne out by the findings of the US Strategic Bombing Survey. Recent assertions to the contrary note the fact that German production remained up during late 1944, but they fail to take into account the desperate measures that the Germans took to keep production up. These measures, such as slave labor and radical disbursement of industry, were temporary panaceas at best and the German economy slowed dramatically in early 1945 when essential supplies ran out. Citing the destruction of factories and rail lines by Allied bombing, German Armaments Minister Albert Speer reported on 15 May 1945 that 'the German economy is heading for an inevitable collapse within 4–8 weeks.' By that time, however, the Allied armies had reached Berlin and Germany had surrendered.

Having observed the success of bombers in World War II, all three of the major undefeated Allied powers moved quickly to develop a new generation of bombers.

In Britain, the makers of three of the Royal Air Force's great World War II bombers began work on a new generation of strategic jets that would be known as the V-Bombers. From Avro, who had built the World War II Lancaster, came the Vulcan; from Handley Page, who had given the RAF the Halifax, came the Victor; while Vickers, who had produced the Wellington, began work on its Valiant.

In the United States, it was much the same story. The companies that had dominated the strategic bomber field during the war led the way in the first generation of postwar bombers. Convair, who as Consolidated Vultee had built the War-time B-24, went ahead with the postwar world's first new bomber, the huge B-36. Boeing, builder of the war-era B-17 and

The Soviet Tu-16 Badger *(above left)*, designed in the 1950s, is still in use. The Tu-26 Backfire *(above right)* was the only strategic bomber introduced in the 1970s. While the Soviets deployed new bombers, the B-52 *(below)* served the US for three decades. This B-52 is shown taking off from the sway-backed runway at Anderson AFB.

B-29, began development of the B-47 and B-52.

During World War II, the USSR had experimented with strategic aircraft, but placed its emphasis almost entirely on the deployment of tactical aircraft. After the war, having seen the effects of American and British bombing on Germany, the Soviets began work on their own first generation of postwar bombers. The first was Tupolev's Tu-4 (NATO codename 'Bull') which was an almost exact copy of the Boeing B-29, and thus it is not really to be considered of the postwar generation. The Tu-4 was, however, followed by the Tu-20/Tu-95 (NATO codename 'Bear'), a truly outstanding four-turbo-prop long-range bomber, and the Tu-16 (NATO codename 'Badger'), a smaller twin jet bomber. While the Tupolev design bureau would come to dominate the Soviet bomber field, the Myasishchev

Mya-4 (NATO codename 'Bison') made an auspicious appearance, leading many observers to regard it as the Soviet equal to the American B-52. Though it would later be shown to have many serious design flaws, the Mya-4 stands as the largest non-American all-jet bomber of the first postwar generation.

In addition to these nine major postwar bombers, many other prototype projects were developed to the flight-test stage. Many smaller bombers were also developed and placed into squadron service by the three major powers and by other nations as well. These included the North American B-45, Martin B-57 and Douglas B-66 (A3D in US Navy service) in the United States; the Ilyushin Il-28 in the Soviet Union; and the English Electric Canberra.

All of these aircraft were developed and deployed in the first ten years after World War II, hence the term 'first generation.' They all combined the strategic concepts developed during the war with the technological developments (such as jet power) that were a result of the blizzard of research and development that followed the war.

In the second decade to follow the war, far fewer new bomber types were placed into squadron service. The United States introduced the Convair B-58, the Soviet Union the Tupolev Tu-22, and France fielded the Dassault-Breguet Mirage IV. Britain introduced no second-generation bombers.

By the 1955–65 period, it had become clear to air warfare planners that the strategic air power concepts developed during World War II had become obsolete. The nature of warfare had changed. The size and scope of the conflicts were much smaller, and the distances involved in air combat activities were shorter than many of those in World War II, and a good deal shorter than the capabilities of first-generation bombers. Meanwhile, smaller attack aircraft became capable of carrying as big a bomb load as the World War II heavy bombers.

Another factor that changed the way planners looked at strategic air warfare was the advent of nuclear weapons. If truly long-range strategic bombing were ever to be used again as part of total war, the horrible destructive power of nuclear weapons would result in near-complete annihilation of the combatants. For the major nuclear powers, the United States and the Soviet Union, land-and-sea-based intercontinental missiles became more important as potential delivery systems for nuclear weapons. For both of these countries, first-generation bombers provided the backbone of the bomber fleet for more than twenty years, long after they should have been considered obsolete. Britain, meanwhile, was phasing out its bomber fleet, content to rest under the American nuclear umbrella, while France developed the relatively small Mirage IV simply to retain a fully independent delivery system for its nuclear arsenal.

While over a dozen new bomber types were introduced into squadron service worldwide in the first decade after the Second World War, only three (the B-58, Tu-22 and Mirage IV) were introduced in the second decade. In the third decade (1965-75), the United States added only a bomber version of the F-111 fighter designated FB-111. The fourth decade leading into the 1980s proved to be the most important period of bomber development since 1955.

By the mid-1970s, both the United States and the Soviet Union were developing their first large, long-range heavy bombers since the first generation. For the United States it was the Rockwell B-1, while across the globe the Soviets were preparing to deploy the Tupolev Tu-26

Above: The F-105 'Thud' saw more actual combat than any other US second-generation warplane.

Below: The P-51 *(left)* of World War II had a bubble canopy and high maneuverability which resurfaced in the likes of the fourth-generation F-16.

(NATO codename 'Backfire'). The two planes were similar in many ways. They were both large aircraft; the biggest warplanes, in fact, to be produced in a quarter century. They were also similar in overall layout, with their most distinctive feature being a variable-geometry wing system that allowed the sweep of the wings to be altered.

The major difference between the B-1 and the Backfire was that while the latter was deployed as planned, the B-1 program was canceled by President Jimmy Carter. When the 1980s began, the front line Soviet bombers were Backfires, less than five years old, while the first line

American bombers were the 20 to 25-year-old B-52s. Meanwhile, the Tupolev design bureau was working on a still more sophisticated aircraft (NATO codename 'Blackjack') to succeed the Backfire. In response to this, the United States revived the B-1 program, which resulted in the deployment of a greatly updated B-1B. When the B-1B entered service in 1985, it was the first new bomber type to do so anywhere during the 1980s.

THE EVOLUTION OF FIGHTERS

Insofar as tactical air power is the basic building block of a modern air force, the fighter is the basic component of tactical air power. By definition, a fighter is a relatively small, fast and highly maneuverable aircraft whose primary mission is to fight other aircraft, and whose secondary mission is to engage enemy surface forces on the battlefront. In its primary role, the fighter is charged with the task of achieving air superiority over a battlefield. Once this is achieved, tactical air power can turn its attention to air-to-surface battlefield support missions.

Traditionally, tactical battlefield support activities are provided by two types of aircraft: fighter-bombers and attack aircraft. The former are simply fighters equipped to carry bombs, while the latter are aircraft in the same size and weight class, but which are slower and more specifically designed to deliver a particular type of ordnance. Up through World War II, there were a number of specialized types of attack aircraft such as torpedo bombers and dive bombers. After the war, with aircraft and ordnance becoming more and more sophisticated, the concept of multirole aircraft developed. One model of a given aircraft might be specifically tailored for use as an air-superiority

bombers, the first generation of postwar fighters in the United States was dominated by the manufacturers that had produced the cream of the wartime fighter crop. Lockheed produced the P-80 (F-80 after 1948) and the F-94; Republic the F-84 series; and North American produced the notable F-86 Sabre Jet series. Meanwhile, both Grumman and Vought produced jet fighters for the US Navy. In the Soviet Union, the design bureaus of Yakovlev and Mikoyan-Gurevich began to develop a first generation of jet fighters based in part on captured German designs.

Whereas only three nations had set about to develop a postwar bomber generation, there was a wide proliferation of nations that would initiate jet fighter programs. The reasons were several. There was a perceived need to bring one's national aviation industry into the jet age, and fighters, being relatively small and compact, were a good place to start. Furthermore, for most nations, territorial air defense and short-range attack operations would be the extent of their need for combat aircraft. Both Britain and France, of course, were early entrants in the jet fighter's first generation, but many other countries joined as well. In Sweden, Saab began work on the first in a series of jet fighters that would provide the traditionally neutral Swedes with modern and domestically produced air combat capability for the next 40 years. The first decade after World War II also saw a number of countries, such as Canada and Switzerland, developing their only home-grown jet fighters. At the same time, both Spain and India imported top wartime German designers to help them build their first-generation jet fighters. Germany, who had pioneered operational jet fighters in 1944, had also lost the war and was not to have a viable combat aircraft industry for 20 years.

The second generation of postwar fighters, like the second generation of postwar bombers, was marked by consolidation. Fewer companies in fewer countries were building jet fighters. In the Soviet Union, the Yakovlev design bureau declined in importance while the Mikoyan-Gurevich bureau ascended to the point where their prefix, MiG, came to be almost synonymous with Soviet fighters. The Sukhoi bureau grew in importance as well.

In France, Dassault's Etendard and Mirage series became the mainstays of both the French air force and of the growing French arms-for-export industry. In Britain, mergers reduced the number of companies until they were all finally funneled into government-owned British Air-

fighter, while another model might be designed as a fighter-bomber, and the third as a high-altitude interceptor. It would be the same basic airframe with detail differences.

In terms of evolution, postwar fighters can be grouped into generations in much the same way we did with bombers. The first generation, appearing in the first decade after the war, was marked by a near-complete conversion to jet power. During World War II, only Germany was able to field jet fighters in combat operations, but both the United States and Britain had

From bottom: First-generation F-84 Thunderstreaks on a snow-covered Alaskan runway; a trio of sleek second-generation F-106 Delta Darts passing over Alaska's Mt McKinley; a third-generation F-4 Phantom over a castle on the Rhine River.

Opposite: Two fourth-generation Tornado GRMk.1s, from 9 Squadron, RAF Honington, carrying four 1000 lb bombs, two full tanks and two ECM pods.

such aircraft in well-advanced stages of flight testing. In fact, both the American Lockheed P-80 and the British Gloster Meteor became operational within a few months of the end of the war. As with

(BAC), which would later become British Aerospace (BAe).

In the United States, the second generation of postwar fighters was typified by the US Air Force 'Century series,' so named because they coincidentally began with the North American F-100. The Century series fighters were developed by different manufacturers and were themselves very different aircraft, but they had several things in common. Most notably, emphasis was on speed and performance. The Century series fighters flew higher and faster than any similar group of operational fighters before them.

The third generation of American jet fighters were those which arrived in service simultaneously with the Defense Department's tri-service designation system, that merged the separate Army, Navy and Air Force aircraft designation nomenclature in 1962. Under the new system, the USAF Century series retained its designations (F-100 through F-109), but the Navy redesignated its existing aircraft

under the new system, which restarted at 1. For fighters, the F-1 through F-3 went to first-generation Navy fighters, and F-6, F-7, F-9, F-10 and F-11 went to existing Navy second-generation fighters.

The third-generation fighters would be in the forefront of American combat activities during the long war in Southeast Asia.

Both the US Navy and US Air Force had two third-generation fighters. For the Navy it was the McDonnell F-4 Phantom and the Vought F-8 Crusader. The USAF's General Dynamics F-111 took no new designation, but the McDonnell F-110 Phantom, virtually identical to the Navy's F-4, became F-4 in Air Force service as well.

Although it would not be known publicly for 26 years, the pre-1962 nomenclature system was retained for classified projects and secret test programs of foreign hardware. The first of these made public was the Lockheed F-117 stealth fighter whose existence was acknowledged in 1988.

THE FOURTH GENERATION

As had been the case with the earlier generations of combat aircraft, warplanes of the fourth generation have important elements in common. In the intense air combat environments of Southeast Asia and the Middle East during the late 1960s and early 1970s several factors were demonstrated that would affect the design of the fourth postwar generation. It was shown that higher speeds did not necessarily enhance an aircraft's combat capabilities. Dogfights were taking place at the same speeds as they had during the Korean War. Too much emphasis had been placed on raw performance rather than tailoring the aircraft to the mission. The absence of an internal gun and overreliance on air-to-air missiles, for example, proved to be a major deficiency when the F-4 Phantom first went into combat in Vietnam.

Lack of maneuverability was another key deficiency. In World War II and Korea, maneuverability was taken for granted, but in the second and third generations of jet fighters it had been sacrificed in favor of speed.

These lessons were applied to warplanes worldwide. In the United States, for example, the new aircraft introduced between the mid-1970s and early 1980s included the F-14 and F-18 for the Navy and the F-15 and F-16 for the Air Force. Each of these aircraft embodies technical improvements that have both altered and enhanced American air combat strategy and practice.

Another important change in the development of combat aircraft to come into maturity in the 1980s was the advent of multinational cooperative efforts. Typically, such aircraft were second-echelon aircraft, such as light attack aircraft, which could also serve as trainers, or vice-versa. As such, they were relatively less complex and less expensive than first-echelon fighters and could be developed for export as well as home use. An early example was the SEPECAT Jaguar, a cooperative effort of BAe in Britain and Breguet in France. More typical was the slower and simpler Alpha Jet developed jointly by Dassault-Breguet in France and Dornier in West Germany. In addition to service with France, West Germany and Belgium, the Alpha Jet has been exported to several nations in Africa and the Middle East. Other recent cooperative efforts have included the AMX developed by Aeritalia and Aermacchi in Italy and Embraer in Brazil, and the ORAO/IAR.93, which is a joint effort of Soko in Yugoslavia and CNIAR in Romania.

The multinational trend also led to development of the Tornado, a decidedly first-line fighter/fighter-bomber by Panavia, an international consortium consisting of Aeritalia, British Aerospace and West Germany's Messerschmitt-Bölkow-Blohm. Transatlantic cooperation has led to the British Aerospace Harrier being co-produced *and* co-developed by McDonnell Douglas in the United States.

In Europe, the multinational trend will come to be the rule rather than the exception as the 1992 unification of European markets becomes a practical, rather than theoretical, reality. Indeed, ventures such as Panavia and the Eurofighter consortium formed in 1986 will become models that are applicable to other industries.

When one ponders a machine as huge and powerful as a modern warplane, it is hard to imagine that one of the most important features separating warplanes of the 1990s from their cousins of the 1960s is the tiny microchip. The same

Above: Fitted with AGM-65 Maverick missiles and the Pave Penny laser spot tracker pod, the F-16 fighter becomes the A-16 attack bomber.

microchip revolution that put personal computers into millions of homes and five-dollar digital time pieces onto millions of wrists also revolutionized the systems under the skin of modern warplanes. The early electronic navigational and aiming systems in aircraft relied on heavy and cumbersome hardware with large vacuum tubes and other heavy gear. It is axiomatic that a footlocker full of vacuum tube electronics could be replaced by a handful of transistors or a microchip smaller than a postage stamp.

Such miniaturization has not only permitted aircraft to become more sophisticated, it has greatly increased the ease by which they can be updated. In the early postwar years, electronic systems were wired into an aircraft. If they required updating, the plane had to be rewired. In

the 1960s systems hardware was built into modules or 'black boxes' that could be pulled out and replaced with other systems. The software revolution of the 1980s now makes the upgrading of an aircraft's systems as easy as replacing a chip or software cartridge.

Particularly in American warplanes, Very High Speed Integrated Circuitry (VHSIC) has permitted more electronic systems to be put into smaller spaces than ever, changing aircraft design forever. The systems themselves have greatly enhanced the aircraft's operational capability.

The Head-Up Display (HUD), now common on many modern Western warplanes, projects essential data on a transparent screen inside the canopy so that the pilot does not have to look down at his altimeter or fuel gauge during a critical moment of a dogfight.

Forward-Looking Infrared (FLIR) systems permit nighttime vision with nearly

the same clarity as broad daylight. The new Low-Altitude Navigation and Targeting Infrared for Night (LANTIRN) system began making is appearance on American fighter-bombers in the mid-1980s. As both a navigation and targeting system, LANTIRN permits ground-attack operations in almost any weather.

Another important factor from a pilot's point of view that has been addressed in fourth-generation fighters has been cockpit visibility. The bubble canopies introduced in the middle of World War II gave pilots a great field of view, but gradually designers forgot their wartime lessons as the emphasis came to be more on speed than dogfighting. In terms of cockpit visibility, the point can be made by comparing the F-4 to the F-15, the F-106 to the F-16 or the MiG-25 to the MiG-29. As can be seen in the comparison of a P-51 and an F-16 on page nine, bubble canopies have come full circle.

Above: The Lockheed F-117A Nighthawk first flew in 1981, but its shape and appearance were kept secret until 1988. The US Air Force ordered 59 of these mysterious fighter-bombers, which employ stealth technology to make themselves invisible to enemy search radar and weapons targeting radar. Even in the 1990s the Air Force has revealed few details about the F-117.

Inside the cockpit things have changed as well. The voice-activated controls tested on the AFTI/F-16 in the 1980s are becoming practical.

The evolution of aircraft systems has gone hand in glove with the evolution of tactics. Once it was proven in the 1960s that surface-to-air missiles (SAMs) could shoot down high-flying aircraft, the tactics changed. Aircraft started flying closer to the ground and systems were developed to make it possible for aircraft—and cruise missiles as well—to fly literally at tree-top level. A major innovation of the 1980s was 'look-down/shoot-down' radar, which made it possible for the first time for a higher flying aircraft to

use radar to look down into the 'ground clutter' caused by trees and hills and to target low-flying craft from above. This led in turn to stealth technology, as aircraft designers sought to entirely eliminate the threat of being seen on radar.

Stealth technology (described in detail in the context of the Northrop B-2 on pages 108 through 111) has become one of the most touted breakthroughs in the fourth generation of warplanes. It has become so important that it has radically changed the way aircraft are designed, both in terms of process and final configuration. The importance of the latter is underscored by the heavy security that surrounded the development of the B-2 and F-117. These two are the only known aircraft which are designed specifically *as* stealth aircraft, but aspects of stealth technology are expected to be part of the essential design requirements for most members of the now forthcoming fifth generation of warplanes.

BRITISH AEROSPACE/McDONNELL DOUGLAS
HARRIER

A MOST UNUSUAL AIRCRAFT

In the midst of the post-World War II aviation technology boom, it had been a dream of engineers and air-power tacticians alike to develop a combat aircraft that functioned like a conventional aircraft while in flight, but which could take off and land vertically! Several prototypes of such aircraft were built in many countries in the 1950s and 1960s, with most major manufacturers rejecting the notion as impractical. Two firms, however, continued unabated. In the lead was Britain's Hawker Aircraft. Several paces behind was the Soviet Yakovlev design bureau, which kept a watchful eye on the Hawker project.

The Hawker project was based on the Bristol BE.52 engine that incorporated the theory of vectoring the engine thrust downward, which had been developed by Frenchman Michel Wibault. Despite a NATO request for Vertical/Short Take Off & Landing (V/STOL) designs, the British government was rather cool to the idea, and Hawker proceeded on its own. In late 1959, however, the British Ministry of Supply advanced some money toward the cost of the prototypes then under construction under the company

designation P.1127. The first vertical flight test of the new aircraft with its 11,000 lb thrust Bristol engine (now called Pegasus 2) took place in October 1960, with test pilot Bill Bedford taking off vertically and hovering for nearly two hours. After a number of hovering tests the P.1127 made its first conventional flight in March 1961.

After the initial success, a group of production P.1127s (now named Kestrel) were ordered by the Royal Air Force (RAF) to form an evaluation squadron in 1965. The Kestrel evaluation was, however, disbanded after having helped prove the validity of the tactical V/STOL concept. Hawker continued work on the project, having received an RAF order for an upgraded version of the Kestrel, now to be called Harrier. The first flight of a pre-production Harrier GR Mk1 came on 31 August 1966, with the first production Harrier Mk1 making its maiden flight on 28 December 1968. In 1969, the US government approved the purchase of 12 Harriers and the long-term acquisition of 110 more for the US Marine Corps under the designation AV-8A.

Between 4 and 11 May 1969, RAF Harriers took part in the Daily Mail Transatlantic Air Race from London to New

Below: A Royal Air Force Harrier GR3 taking off vertically from a highway in Germany.

Bottom left: A US Marine Corps AV-8A Harrier II.

Above right: Next to the top-view silhouette of the
Harrier are the military insignias of the user nations.
From left to right: India, Spain, the United Kingdom and
the United States.

Hawker Project 1127   British Aerospace Harrier GR Mk1 (single seat)   British Aerospace Harrier T Mk2 (two-seat, shown here with external stores)   British Aerospace/McDonnell Douglas Harrier II

York. Though he set no transatlantic speed records with his 6-hour-12-minute crossing, RAF Squadron Leader Tom Lecky-Thompson did establish an important milestone when he used the Harrier's vertical landing capability to become the first man to successfully land a jet fighter within Manhattan.

By July 1969, Harriers were in RAF squadron service and a year later the two-seat Harrier Mk2 trainers were in service. In November 1972, British Aerospace, which by now had absorbed Hawker Aircraft, received a study contract for the Royal Navy, which envisioned small Harrier-equipped aircraft carriers as an economical replacement for large, full-sized carriers. Three years later the Royal Navy placed an order for 24 naval versions which would be known as Sea Harrier FRS Mk1. In the same year, the Spanish navy ordered 6 Harriers and 2 Harrier trainers under the American AV-8 designation.

Also in 1975 McDonnell Douglas and the USMC jointly began development, under license from British Aerospace, of an advanced Harrier that would be built by the McDonnell component of McDonnell Douglas at St Louis under the designation AV-8B. The AV-8B Harrier II differed from the Hawker Siddeley (now part of British Aerospace) version with the addition of a graphite epoxy wing, having a supercritical airfoil for greater lift, better cruise characteristics and much greater fuel capacity. Redesigned engine inlets and new fuselage-mounted lift-improvement devices resulted in greater lift for improved take off, landing and cruise performance.

Meanwhile, in the Soviet Union, the

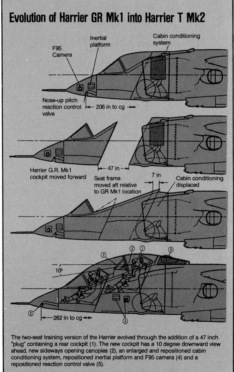

Evolution of Harrier GR Mk1 into Harrier T Mk2

The two-seat training version of the Harrier evolved through the addition of a 47 inch "plug" containing a rear cockpit (1). The new cockpit has a 10 degree downward view ahead, new sideways opening canopies (2), an enlarged and repositioned cabin conditioning system, repositioned inertial platform and F95 camera (4) and a repositioned reaction control valve (5).

Yakovlev Yak-36 (NATO codename 'Forger') V/STOL fighter-bomber made its appearance with the fleet air arm of the Soviet navy. Though similar in appearance to the Harrier, the Yak-36 cannot emulate the Harrier's performance range.

In May 1977, the first of the Royal Navy's V/STOL carriers (officially known as command cruisers), HMS *Invincible*, was launched. The *Invincible* had a 20,000-ton displacement versus the 50,000-ton displacement of HMS *Ark Royal*, the last British conventional carrier. As such, it was less than a quarter the size of modern US Navy attack carriers such as the USS *Nimitz*, which displaces 90,000 tons. The first of the new Sea Har-

riers made its initial flight on 20 August 1978 and joined squadron service on 18 June of the following year.

Meanwhile, across the globe in St Louis, Missouri, the McDonnell Douglas AV-8B Harrier II flight test prototype (designated YAV-8B) made its first flight on 9 November 1978. On 26 February 1982, a joint manufacturing agreement was signed between McDonnell Douglas and British Aerospace, under which they would co-produce 328 Harrier IIs for the US Marine Corps, and 62 for the Royal Air Force.

Less than three months later the British Harriers were sent into combat in the Falklands War, where they were to distinguish themselves beyond expectations. While they were originally conceived more as attack planes than fighters, the Harriers performed brilliantly as air-superiority fighters, making them one of the top combat-tested warplanes of the 1980s.

THE HARRIER IN DETAIL

The heart of any aircraft is its engine, but in the case of the V/STOL Harrier, it is the part of the plane that sets it apart from almost any other aircraft in the world. The engine is a Rolls-Royce Pegasus turbofan, developing over 20,000 lb of thrust which is directed through four rotatable nozzles located under the wings of the aircraft. In a conventional jet aircraft, the thrust is directed straight back and the aircraft is directed, or vectored, forward. In the case of the Harrier, however, the thrust direction, and hence the direction of the aircraft, can be changed by rotating the nozzles with an air motor driven by engine-compressor delivery air. By directing the nozzles

Above: A Royal Air Force Harrier GR3 emerging from its 'hide' in Germany. Two RAF Harrier I squadrons operate in Germany, close to the border for rapid intervention. Off-base hides are used to position Harriers close to possible battle areas. The GR3 is the most advanced British Aerospace Harrier I.

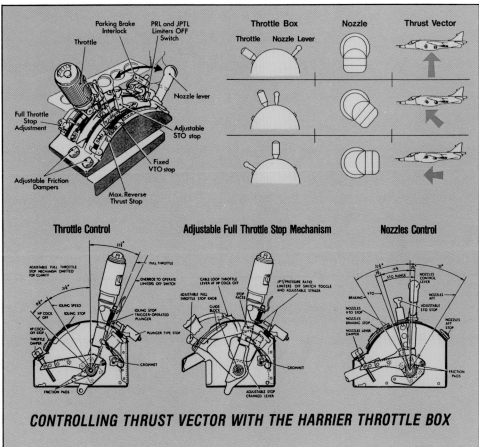

CONTROLLING THRUST VECTOR WITH THE HARRIER THROTTLE BOX

toward the ground and opening the throttle, the pilot can cause the aircraft to lift straight up in a vertical takeoff, or VTO. Once off the ground, the nozzles are rotated aft 90 degrees and the aircraft achieves conventional forward wingborne flight. It is then controlled and operated like a conventional jet. The transition process takes less than 20 seconds and uses less than 100 lb of fuel.

The Harrier's VTO capability is the major operational characteristic that it has to offer the modern air tactician. It can operate from virtually any level patch of ground. It has been demonstrated in recent conflicts that warplanes can be effectively put out of action by the destruction of their airfields, even if the aircraft themselves are untouched. If such a vulnerable airfield component as a runway is put out of service, planes on the ground cannot take off, and planes returning to base cannot land. Neither of these problems would confound a Harrier pilot, whose operating capabilities would be unaffected by the condition of the runway. For a naval air arm, the Harrier's characteristics make it an ideal aircraft because it can land on virtually any type of ship.

While the Harrier's VTO capabilities distinguish it among other warplanes, VTOs use a good deal of fuel. In response to this, a Harrier can make a short takeoff (STO) using the wing along with vectored nozzle for lift, thus saving fuel. To save even more fuel or lift a heavier weapons load a Harrier

may, where possible, make a conventional takeoff utilizing the full length of a runway. An STO begins with the nozzles directed aft, as in a normal takeoff, but by briefly rotating the nozzles to 45 degrees, it allows for takeoff in a much shorter space.

A recent development in STO technology for the Harrier is the 'Ski-Jump' Launch, which consists of a curved ramp at the forward end of the flight deck of the Royal Navy's V/STOL carriers. When launched from the 'Ski-Jump,' the aircraft leaves the deck at a much lower speed

than would be required for a flat-deck takeoff at the same gross weight. The initial upward trajectory from the ramp curves toward the horizontal, allowing the aircraft roughly 10 seconds in which to accelerate to a speed at which the lifting forces equal the aircraft weight. From this point in the launch, the pilot completes a normal transition from vectored downward thrust to wingborne flight by slowly rotating the engine nozzles fully aft. This process permits a 60 percent reduction in deck length required, or an increase of 30 percent plus in military payload capacity over a conventional flat flight deck. Because of the lower speed required, there is an increase in fuel savings. The effects of ship pitching motion on STO launches can be severe, but with the Ski-Jump ship, pitch motion allowance can be reduced because the aircraft's initial trajectory is always away from the sea.

The Harrier is, of course, capable of a conventional landing, but Vertical Land- ings (VL) are actually considered easier and safer. The pilot simply rotates the nozzles to the downward position and the Harrier hovers on the cushion of air that is created. By throttling back, the pilot decreases the thrust using the throttle as the height control, and the plane gently settles down to the ground. While the Harrier is being lowered, delicate ma- neuvers are possible which permit the air- craft to be landed on a precise position.

This is particularly useful in shipboard landings.

Vectoring of the nozzles is by no means restricted to takeoffs and landings. As was demonstrated in the Falklands War, Vectoring In Forward Flight (VIFF) proved to be one of the most important capabili- ties in the Harrier's unique repertoire. By 'VIFFing,' the Harrier could literally stop in mid-air. When pursued by an enemy aircraft, a Harrier pilot would abruptly slow down, allow the attacker to over- shoot him, then speed up and go on the attack. It was demonstrated both in the Falklands War and in simulated air com- bat since that the Harrier can easily out- maneuver all conventional fighter aircraft types against which it is flown.

Inside the Harrier's pressurized cockpit —which has been enlarged in the Sea Harrier and Harrier II variants—flight, navigation, attack and weapon-aiming in- formation is presented to the pilot as a Head-Up Display (HUD) in which the data is projected onto the inside of the wind- screen. A Centralized Warning System (CWS) provides the pilot with audio and/or visual indication of aircraft sys- tem failures, or other problems. Primary warnings involve red light and audible tones in the pilot's headset, while the secondary warnings consist of amber 'captioned window' lights.

The weapons system of the Sea Harrier revolves around the new Ferranti Blue Fox (Blue Vixen in Sea Harrier FRS2, intro- duced in 1986) radar which feeds air or

Above: Three Royal Air Force Harrier GR3s of Number 1 Squadron (based at RAF Wittering in the United Kingdom) were photographed during a weapons training exercise in Sardinia.

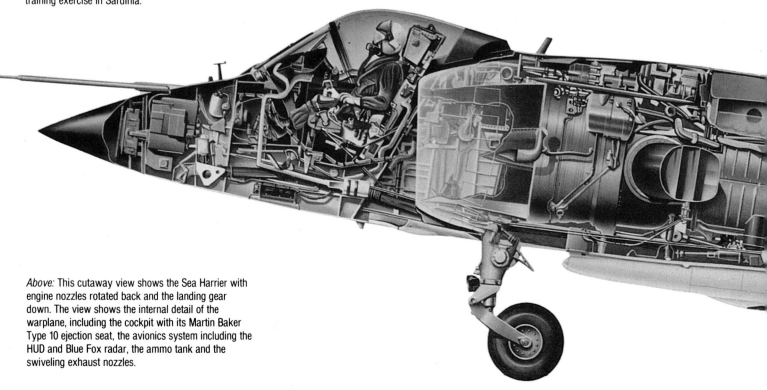

Above: This cutaway view shows the Sea Harrier with engine nozzles rotated back and the landing gear down. The view shows the internal detail of the warplane, including the cockpit with its Martin Baker Type 10 ejection seat, the avionics system including the HUD and Blue Fox radar, the ammo tank and the swiveling exhaust nozzles.

BRITISH AEROSPACE / McDONNELL DOUGLAS HARRIER

	British Aerospace GR3 Harrier	British Aerospace FRS 1 Sea Harrier	McDonnell Douglas/British Aerospace GR5 Harrier II
Year first deployed:	1966	1978	1984
Type:	V/STOL single-seat close-support aircraft	Carrier-based V/STOL support aircraft	V/STOL close-support and reconnaissance aircraft
Power Plant:	One Rolls-Royce Pegasus 103 vectored-thrust turbofan @ 21,500 lb thrust	One Rolls-Royce Pegasus 104 afterburning turbofan @ 21,500 lb thrust	One Rolls-Royce Pegasus 105 afterburning turbofan @ 21,750 lb thrust
Wingspan:	25 ft 3 in	25 ft 3 ft	30 ft 4 in
Length:	46 ft 10 in	47 ft 7 in	46 ft 4 in
Height:	11 ft 11 in	12 ft 2 in	11 ft 8 in
Wing Area:	201 sq ft	201 sq ft	230 sq ft
Gross Weight:	25,200 lb	26,200 lb	29,750 lb
Empty Weight:	13,535 lb	13,444 lb	14,647 lb
Maximum Speed:	Mach 1.3 @ altitude	Mach 1.3 @ altitude	Mach 1.1 @ altitude
Range:	57 mi vertical T-O; 414 mi short T-O	300 mi strike; 400 mi intercept	600 mi strike; 2000 mi ferry
Service Ceiling:	55,000 ft	55,000 ft	55,000 ft
Fixed Armament:	None	Two Aden 30mm cannons or two 25mm cannons	Two Aden 30mm cannons
Users:	Spain, United Kingdom, USMC	India, United Kingdom (Royal Navy)	Spain, United Kingdom, USMC

Left: Three Sea Harriers of 801 Naval Air Squadron in formation. The trident logo of 801 NAS is visible on the Harriers' tails.

Below: Two Sea Harriers of 801 Naval Air Squadron. An acquisition (training) Sidewinder missile can be seen on the farther aircraft's outer starboard weapon pylon. The 801 NAS was the unit that operated from the Royal Navy carrier *Invincible* during the Falklands War.

Right: The Spanish Navy's Harrier II AV-8B is known as Matador.

Right below: An AV-8B undergoing climatic tests at 60 degrees below zero. Four inches of rain were poured and blown on the airframe, and then frozen. The Harrier passed with flying colors.

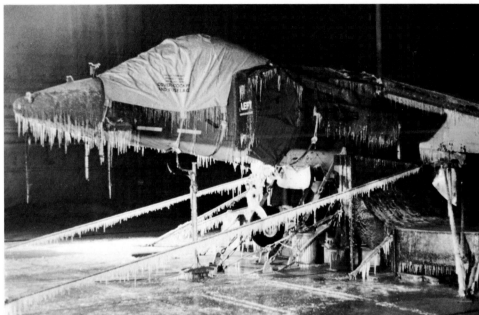

surface target information to a digital Weapon Aiming Computer (WAC) and the HUD. The Blue Fox is an I-Band, pulse-modulated radar designed for airborne interception, as well as air-to-surface search and strike. It provides to the HUD and WAC such data as target range and bearing, scanner azimuth and elevation angles, and angle rates for use in target interception and weapon-aiming equations. The pilot may select from a variety of Blue Fox operating modes:

• Search and detection of air or surface targets
• Target tracking
• Air-to-surface ranging
• Radar lock-on to visual targets
• Navigation

Interfacing with the Blue Fox, the HUD/WAC provides the pilot with a windscreen display of altitude, heading, angle of attack, side force, vertical and forward speed, and barometric or radar attitude. Other operational displays on the HUD include Tactical Air Navigation (TACAN), Ultra-High Frequency (UHF) homing, air-to-air weapon aiming in manual and automatic release modes, and air-to-surface weapon aiming.

The Harrier's Navigation, Heading, and Attitude Reference System (NavHARS) consists of an all-attitude, twin-gyro, three-accelerometer platform to measure attitude and acceleration, and a computer to control navigation computation. Taking 120 seconds to align either ashore or at sea, the NavHARS displays:

• Wind speed and wind direction
• Ground speed and ground track
• Present position in either longitude/latitude, or in reference to a tactical grid
• Range and bearing to TACAN station
• Range, bearing, course and time-to-go to a choice of ten route points
• Time-remaining estimates based on monitoring fuel-flow and fuel reserves

The McDonnell Douglas/British Aerospace Harrier II offers a number of cockpit improvements over the Harrier I. When viewing the two cockpits side by side, the first thing that one notices is a clearer field of vision with the one-piece windscreen and larger canopy. Scanning downward, one sees that all the essential communication, identification and weapons control functions are now located in a single, easy-to-reach panel directly

below the HUD. A multipurpose, digital Cathode Ray Tube (CRT) display on the left has replaced a clutter of dials and gauges and a moving map display is included on the right (RAF GR Mk5 only) as an added navigational aid. The cockpit layout is designed to accommodate added and improved systems as they are developed.

The Sea Harrier's armament begins with two fuselage-mounted pods containing 30mm Aden cannons, and five weapons pylons (two under each wing and one on the fuselage centerline). The two inboard wing pylons can accommodate fuel tanks or a ton of armaments each. The outboard pylons can each carry 1000 lb of armament. The choice of possible weapons is broad and includes a wide spectrum of US, UK and NATO standard bombs, cluster weapons, rockets, flares and air-to-air missiles. The standard armament includes the AIM-9L Sidewinder air-to-air missile, and the Sea Eagle anti-ship missile, but the Sea Harrier is also compatible with Harpoon, Magic and Martel.

The Harrier II armament begins with a single 25mm high-velocity cannon and seven weapons pylons (three on each

Left: US Marine Corps AV-8B Harrier IIs aboard the US Navy's USS *Nassau* (LHA-4).

Below: Each Royal Navy V/STOL carrier has a Ski-Jump Launch at the forward end of its flight deck. Here a Sea Harrier is in launch position.

wing and on the fuselage centerline). These pylons can carry 16 Mk-82 bombs, 6 Mk-83 bombs, 6 BL-755 cluster bombs, four AGM-65 Maverick air-to-ground missiles, four AIM-9L Sidewinder air-to-air missiles, 10 rocket pods, and four fuel tanks for a total external payload of 4.6 tons.

THE HARRIER IN SERVICE

The Harrier first entered service with the RAF in 1969 (GR1), with the US Marine Corps in 1976 (AV-8A), with the Royal Navy in 1979 (Sea Harrier), and the Indian Navy in 1983 (Sea Harrier). The Harrier II first went into service with the US Marine Corps on 16 January 1984 under the designation AV-8B.

At the start of 1985 the Royal Air Force had 57 Harriers in service, with two squadrons in service in Germany, one flight in Belize, and one in the Falklands. The Royal Navy had 26 Sea Harriers in four squadrons, two on carriers, and two in training, with another 14 on order. The US Marine Corps had 45 Harriers in three fighter/ground attack squadrons, another 8 aircraft as trainers, and 33 AV-8Bs on order. The Indian Navy had 8 (of 18 on order) Sea Harriers in service. The Spanish Navy had 9 AV-8As, which it calls Matador, in service, and another 12 AV-8Bs on order.

THE HARRIER AT WAR

An important part of military planning, whether it be in strategy and tactics or in hardware development, is to anticipate the unexpected. By definition, this is difficult and often impossible. So it was in April 1982, when Britain's military establishment found itself forced to fight

Top: An RAF GR3 Harrier in action, probably firing SNEB rockets from a Matra 155 launch pod.

Second from top: Sea Harriers and maintenance crew on the hangar deck of a Royal Navy carrier.

Above: Camouflage nets prevent Harriers positioned in German forests from being spotted from the air.

Above: An RN Sea Harrier makes a Ski Jump take-off as it goes on a mission over the Falklands.

Right: A Sea Harrier of 800 NAS, with all squadron markings painted over. The '14' is used as identification on board the carrier. Three 'kill' marks are visible beneath the cockpit.

Argentina in the Falkland Islands. Because air power is essential in the conduct of modern warfare, the effort to retake the islands captured by the Argentines required such a presence. Because there were no airfields within tactical range of the Falklands, and because the Royal Navy no longer had conventional aircraft carriers, all eyes turned to the Harrier. The RAF's Vulcan strategic bombers would fly a handful of missions against the Argentine-held airport at Stanley, but the vast majority of strike missions, all the ground support missions, and all the air-intercept missions would have to be flown by Harriers.

The Argentine invasion of the Falklands took place on 2 April 1982 and the first elements of the Royal Navy's Falklands Task Force (FTF) left the United Kingdom three days later. Prominent among them were the V/STOL carriers HMS *Invincible*, the FTF flagship, and HMS *Hermes*. Including the Harriers that left with the fleet and those flown out while it was enroute, 20 RN Sea Harriers and 8 RAF Harrier GR3s were initially part of the FTF. These 28 aircraft were augmented by 8 Sea Harriers and 6 RAF Harrier GR3s which were trucked south in the Cunard container ship *Atlantic Conveyor*. These 14 aircraft were transferred to the carriers before the *Atlantic Conveyor* itself was attacked by Argentine aircraft on 25 May.

The Sea Harriers, designed for fleet air defense, were equipped to also fly ground-attack missions, while the ground-attack RAF Harriers were adapted for air defense. All the aircraft performed well. At the beginning of each day of the war, 95 percent of the Harriers were ready for action, and 99 percent of all planned missions were flown. These missions included

RAF Harriers played a major role in the Falklands War. *Above*, a GR3 returns to the carrier with empty bomb pylons after a successful mission. A low-level Harrier recon photo *(bottom)* shows damage from a Harrier bomb strike on Argentine positions near Stanley. Royal Navy Sea Harriers and RAF GR3s *(opposite, bottom)* together aboard a Royal Navy carrier.

over 1100 Combat Air Patrol (CAP) sorties and 90 offensive support missions flown by Sea Harriers, while the RAF Harriers flew 125 ground-attack and reconnaissance sorties.

The Harriers began to fly CAP missions as soon as the FTF came within range of the Falklands and Argentine-based enemy aircraft, with the first interception, that of an Argentine 707, occurring on 21 April. The first air attacks on the Falklands, as well as the first Harrier air-to-air victories over Argentine aircraft, came on 1 May. The first loss of a Harrier to ground fire came on 4 May during an air attack on Goose Green. Though 5 Harriers were lost to ground fire during the war, in air-to-air combat they distinguished themselves beyond expectation. Harriers achieved 20 confirmed (and 3 probable) victories, while the Argentines were unable to shoot down a single Harrier in the air-to-air dogfights. The British pilots were aided by the fact that most of Argentina's combat aircraft had to fly all the way from the mainland because the captured Stanley airport was not jet serviceable. There were other factors that contributed to the lopsided success of the British airmen, including their superior training, but a major element was certainly the Harrier itself and its many unique capabilities, such as VIFFing. In his report to Parliament in December 1982, the British Secretary of State for Defence said of the Harrier: 'These aircraft were a major success, showing themselves to be flexible, robust, reliable and effective.'

First Sea Lord, Admiral Sir Henry Leach, went a step further to say, 'Without the Sea Harrier there could have been no Task Force, and recapture of the Falklands would have been beyond Britain's capability.'

GRUMMAN
F-14 TOMCAT

GRUMMAN'S FOURTH-GENERATION CARRIER CAT

During World War II, the cornerstones of the US Navy's carrier-based air fleet were the tenacious warplanes from the Long Island, New York drawing boards of the Grumman company. There was the Grumman TBF Avenger torpedo bomber of course, but the planes for which the firm became so justly famed were the series of ubiquitous 'cats.' When the war started, and for the first long difficult years, the US Navy's first-line fighter was Grumman's F4F Wildcat. Just when the Wildcat seemed ready for obsolescence in 1943, Grumman was ready with the F6F

Hellcat. Had the war continued into 1946 with the planned invasion of Japan, the skies over the heartland of the 'chrysanthemum empire' would have been filled with examples of Grumman's third and last single-place piston-engined air-superiority fighter, the F8F Bearcat. As it was, the F8F and the twin-engined nightfighter,

Top right: Next to the top-view silhouette of the F-14 Tomcat are military insignias of the user nations, Iran *(left)* and the USA.

Below and right: F-14s taking off from the USS *Enterprise* and over the USS *John F Kennedy.*

Right: Prop-driven Grumman cats from the 1940s. *(From top):* The F4F Wildcat and the F6F Hellcat, both of which served in World War II, and the F8F Bearcat.

the F7F Tigercat, became Grumman's first contributions to the postwar Navy.*

With its proud heritage of piston-engined jets firmly in place, Grumman turned to jet fighters. The first of these were the F9F-1 through F9F-5 Panther and F9F-6 through F9F-8 Cougar. The Panther (Grumman Model 79) and Cougar (Grumman Model 93) were nearly identical in overall structure except that the former had straight wings and the latter swept wings. The first-generation F9F jet series was followed by the F11F Tiger, a second-generation carrier jet that also served with the Navy's Blue Angels aerobatic team. First entering service in 1957, it would be the last Grumman fighter to enter service with the Navy for more than a dozen years.*

It was against this backdrop that Grumman responded to the US Navy's request for design specifications within the context of its VFX (Navy Fighter, Experimental) program in 1967. Meanwhile, however, another chain of events was unfolding which would lead to the Navy's decision to develop the VFX project. This series of events revolved around the costly TFX (Tactical Fighter, Experimental) project which had been conceived in the Defense Department during the early 1960s. Defense Secretary Robert McNamara wanted the US Navy and US Air Force to develop common aircraft systems. He had merged their nomenclature systems and he wanted them to have the same new tactical fighter. The result was the General Dynamics F-111 which was ironically the last plane designated under the *old* nomenclature. Theoretically, the same basic aircraft design would meet the needs of both services, but this didn't work. The F-111 was an aircraft of compromise and the compromise gave the Air Force something less than that for which they'd hoped, while the Navy found themselves with a fighter that was not suitable for carrier operations.

The Navy withdrew from the TFX/F-111 project and went its own way, redefining its requirement under the VFX program. Grumman at the same time had been developing a new-generation carrier-

*The Grumman FF (F1F) and F3F were US Navy prewar biplane fighters while the F2F, F5F, F10F (Jaguar) and F12F were experimental projects that never went into production. After the 1962 Department of Defense merger of all services nomenclature systems, the F9F was conveniently redesignated F-9 while the F11F was redesignated F-11. These two types were the only Grumman fighters still in the inventory at that time.

fighter design on its own. This design, Grumman Model 303, was submitted to the Navy in 1968 as a VFX contender. In January 1969 the Grumman entry was chosen over that of McDonnell Douglas.

Because of the time that had been lost because of the TFX, and because of the lessons being learned in the air war in Vietnam, the Navy decided to proceed quickly with its new fighter which was now designated F-14. Because of the involvement of Deputy Chief of Naval Operations for Air, Admiral Tom Connolly, in the project, the F-14 was known informally for some time as 'Tom's cat.' Passing up suggestions such as Alley Cat and Sea Cat, the Navy decided on a variation of the informal nickname and the F-14 became the Tomcat.

Because they had been working on the idea for some time before they officially received the contract, Grumman was able to move relatively quickly with the F-14 project. The first Tomcat flight took place on 21 December 1970, less than two years after the contract was issued. During the second flight 10 days later, the first prototype's hydraulic systems failed. Grumman test pilots Robert Smythe and Bill Miller attempted to coax the big bird in for a landing, but the plane gradually became uncontrollable and they were forced to

eject about a mile from the runway. A simple substitution of steel hydraulic lines for titanium proved to be the solution to the problem, which had been traced to this tubing.

The flight test program was successfully renewed with the same two crewmen flying the second prototype in May 1971. The twelfth prototype was used for the high-speed tests that had been planned for the lost first prototype. On 16 September 1971 this aircraft became the first F-14 to fly at supersonic speed.

Flight testing proceeded in earnest throughout 1972, with weapons and avionics tests taking place at Point Mugu NAS in California. Weapons tests included successful firings of the sophisticated new Phoenix air-to-air missile. The first catapult launch of an F-14 took place on 16 June 1972 aboard the USS *Forrestal* off Chesapeake Bay. This was followed by the first F-14 carrier landing on 28 June. The same aircraft, the tenth prototype, was lost the following day during a low-level test flight mishap over Chesapeake Bay that also claimed the life of test pilot Bill Miller. On the whole, however, the flight tests went smoothly and successfully.

The first two carrier squadrons to receive the F-14 were VF-1 (The *Wolfpack*)

and VF-2 (The *Bounty Hunters*) aboard the USS *Enterprise* on 17 September 1974. Following this first Tomcat deployment into the Pacific, squadrons VF-14 (The *Tophatters*) and VF-32 (The *Swordsmen*) aboard the USS *John F Kennedy* received F-14s for deployment with the Sixth Fleet in the Mediterranean. By the end of 1976, there were six Tomcat squadrons on three carriers in the US Navy and by the end of 1977, the numbers had doubled.

At the same time, Grumman's efforts to sell the Tomcat abroad were not meeting with a great deal of success. In general it was a matter of cost. Grumman and the US Navy had spared no expense in producing the best possible carrier fighter, and as a result found themselves not only with an outstanding fighter but with a very expensive fighter. Furthermore, because the F-14 was developed only as an air-superiority fighter, it was ruled out by potential customers who wanted a secondary ground-attack capability in their fighter. In 1974, one air force for whom money was no object was the Imperial Iranian Air Force of Shah Mohammed Reza Pahlavi. The Shah was at that time determined to make oil-rich Iran into a world superpower with a military force befitting such a power. He was also concerned about Soviet MiG-25s that were

Two F-14 squadrons were first deployed on the nuclear-powered USS *Enterprise* (CVN-65). *Above*, a Tomcat from VF-1 Wolfpack joins its squadron on deck. VF-1 was the first fleet squadron equipped with F-14s. The Wolfpack logo is seen on the F-14 in the foreground. As an F-14 from VF-2 Bounty Hunters *(below)* comes in for a landing, the widely spaced engine pods are visible.

able to overfly Iranian territory because his F-4s were unable to match their performance and intercept them. For this he needed a modern high-performance jet like the F-14 and a sophisticated air-to-air missile like the Phoenix. Not only could the Shah afford these weapons, he helped arrange a loan to Grumman from the Bank Melli Iran in 1974 that helped the Tomcat program survive a post-Vietnam round of congressional budget slashing.

The first 3 of 80 desert-camouflaged F-14s destined for the 'peacock air force' arrived at the military facility of Tehran's Mehrabad Airport on 27 January 1976. In August of the following year testing by F-14s of armed Phoenix missiles resulted in the Soviet Union's halting of its reconnaissance flights. In July of 1978 the last Iranian Tomcat was delivered, but less than a year later the country was swallowed by revolution. In the ensuing confusion, the Iranian air force fell into disarray, and the Grumman technical personnel sent to Iran to help train the air force were forced out. As a result, the air force inherited by the new Islamic Republic of Iran had lost the ability to use its F-14s to their fullest potential.

The US Navy, meanwhile, continued to expand its F-14 fleet. The latest Grumman cat was living up to its proud heritage as it took its perhaps predestined place as the US Navy's top air-superiority fighter for the 1980s.

THE TOMCAT IN DETAIL

The F-14 Tomcat is among the largest fighters to see service in the 1980s, dwarfing many of its deckmates aboard the Navy's carriers. It is most often compared to the US Air Force's top air-superiority fighter, the F-15, with which it has many features in common. The two planes are nearly the same size and both have dual vertical tail surfaces making them similar in appearance. Both are powered by two engines, making them extremely powerful aircraft capable of speeds comfortably above Mach 2. The Tomcat is powered by a pair of Pratt & Whitney TF30 engines such as those developed for the F-111 project. The Navy had planned to ask Grumman for an F-14B aircraft with more powerful Pratt & Whitney F401s similar to the F-15's F100s but the engine developed technical problems and was canceled in April 1974. In 1984 the Air Force announced that it would be buying a mix of Pratt & Whitney F100s and General Electric F110s for its expanding fleet of F-15s and F-16s. The Navy followed suit with the announcement that it would ask Grumman to develop a new-generation F-14D to be powered by the F110 turbofan.

While it has twin engine power in common with the F-15, the F-14 is distinguished from other American fourth-generation aircraft by its two-man crew and its variable-geometry wing. The two-man crew, which includes the pilot and weapons operator, is unusual among fighter aircraft without an established ground-attack capability. The F-14 is also the only American fighter since the F-111 to have variable-geometry wings. The sweep of these wings can be varied from 20 degrees to 60 degrees in flight and can be folded back to 75 degrees on the ground to permit easier storage aboard carriers.

While the primary structural material in the F-14 is aluminum, there is very little use of carbon/epoxy composites as there is in many other new warplanes. By weight, the Tomcat is 36 percent aluminum, 25 percent titanium and just 4 percent non-metallic compounds. The variable-geometry wings of the F-14 differ from those of the F-111, Tornado and MiG-23/27 in that they have no attachment points for weapons. The attachment points are located under the fuselage, under the engine nacelles (for fuel tanks only) and under the large wing root 'glove' in which the wing swivels. When the F-14 is viewed head-on with wings swept, the glove extends more than half way from fuselage to wing tip. It is on the outer edges of the glove that special curved pylons are attached.

While there is no technical reason why it cannot be adapted for air-to-ground munitions, the Tomcat in US Navy service carries only air-to-air weapons. These include the AIM-9 Sidewinder and AIM-7 Sparrow, the standard air-to-air missiles used aboard all American fighters. The F-14 is also capable of launching the AIM-120 AMRAAM (Advanced Medium Range Air-to-Air

GRUMMAN F-14A TOMCAT

Year first deployed:	1972
Type:	Two-seat carrier-based variable-geometry fighter
Power Plant:	Two Pratt & Whitney TF-30-P-414A afterburning turbofans @ 20,900 lb thrust each
Wingspan:	64 ft 2 in spread; 38 ft 2 in swept
Length:	61 ft 11 in
Height:	16 ft
Wing Area:	565 sq ft
Gross Weight:	73,248 lb
Empty Weight:	39,310 lb
Maximum Speed:	Mach 2.3 @ altitude; Mach 1.2 @ sea level
Range:	2,000 mi w/external tanks
Service Ceiling:	56,000 ft
Fixed Armament:	One General Electric M61 20mm Vulcan
Users:	Iran, USN

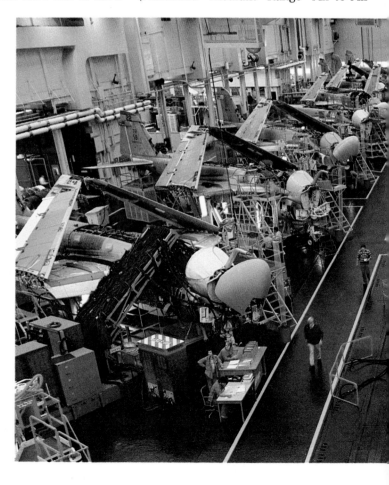

Above: This bottom view of a Tomcat shows six Phoenix missiles. The weapons pylons are located on the massive wing root instead of on the wing.

Below: The Grumman Tomcat assembly line in Bethpage, New York. At left, A-6 Intruders are also under construction for the US Navy.

Missile), but one weapon unique to the F-14 is the AIM-54 Phoenix air-to-air missile. A descendant of the earlier AIM-4 Falcon series, the Phoenix was developed at the same time as the F-14 and is used only aboard the F-14.

While missiles such as the Sidewinder and Sparrow are designed for use at short-to-medium range and in visual-range dogfights, the Phoenix is designed as a high-altitude intercept missile with a 60-mile range at top speed in the Mach 4 region. It was the Phoenix that helped the Shah decide to buy the F-14 and it is the Phoenix that helps make the F-14 such a good fleet interceptor for the US Navy. Tests carried out during the 1970s and early 1980s demonstrated an outstanding 92 percent success rate for the Tomcat/ Phoenix team. The team demonstrated its effectiveness against multiple drones simulating the performance of both fighters and bombers as well as against drones simulating the performance of sea-skimming cruise missiles. The Tomcat can carry up to six AIM-54s and can launch at six targets simultaneously, but normally only four missiles are carried.

In addition to its suite of sophisticated guided weaponry, the Tomcat carries an M61 Vulcan 20mm six-barreled rotary

cannon as fixed armament. The Vulcan is located on the left side of the fuselage, immediately forward of the cockpit.

The avionics systems of the Tomcat revolve around the Hughes AWG-9 doppler radar which is capable of such operating modes as look-down/shoot-down, track-while-scan, range-while-search, single/multiple target-tracking and air-to-ground mapping. Radar counter-measures hardware include the ALQ-91 and ALQ-100 electronic jammers and the ALE-39 chaff dispenser. Later F-14s and F-14Ds are equipped with the ALR-67 and ALQ-165 ASPJ (Advanced Self-Protection Jammer) electronic jamming systems and the ALQ-129 system that is designed to interrupt tracking of the F-14 by surface-to-air missiles.

THE TOMCAT IN SERVICE

Designed for the US Navy and exported only to Iran, the Grumman F-14 Tomcat is in service with fewer air arms than any other major fourth-generation American fighter. The reasons for this are due not only to the aircraft's high cost, but to its high level of specialization in the fighter/interceptor role. By 1978, the Imperial Iranian Air Force (IIAF) had 80 Tomcats organized into four squadrons

with a large number of American technicians in Iran to help these squadrons become fully operational in their complicated new aircraft. A year later the Shah's empire was overthrown and Iran's government was taken over by anti-American Moslem fundamentalists. Many Americans fled the chaos that gripped Iran and 53 US citizens who were not so lucky were kidnaped by terrorists and held for more than a year with the blessing of Iran's new Islamic fundamentalist government. Against this backdrop American technical assistance and the flow of spare parts for Iran's F-14 transition program came to a

halt. While much of the American equipment remained usable for the new Islamic Republic Iran Air Force (IRIAF), this was not true for the F-14 and the sophisticated Phoenix missile.

When Iran went to war with Iraq in the fall of 1980, only a handful of F-14s were usable because of lack of spare parts and qualified pilots. Despite frequent Iraqi claims of F-14s intercepted and shot down, the IRIAF carefully guarded its arsenal's ultimate weapons system. The aircraft were rarely used in actual combat, but rather they were utilized as airborne early-warning aircraft because of

Portraits of Squadron VF-84 Jolly Rogers of the USS *Nimitz:* The skull-and-cross-bones logo is prominent on the above F-14; a pilot is greeted by his son upon return from deployment *(right);* and a pilot at work *(opposite above).*

Left: An F-14 of the Imperial Iranian Air Force.

their sophisticated Hughes AWG-9 radar system. Early in the war, there were unconfirmed reports that the Phoenix missile had been used in combat, but as time goes by it seems less likely that these weapons could have been maintained in operable condition without American technical support. Up to 16 of the original F-14s were kept flyable during the first five years of the Iran-Iraq war by cannibalizing the fleet for spare parts, and by October 1984 there were reports that some parts were being manufactured in Iran. By the beginning of 1985 these 16 Tomcats, which constituted less than one of the original squadrons, were broken into three detachments assigned to tactical air bases at Buchehr, Mehrabad (Tehran) and Shiraz.

The US Navy meanwhile had 20 fighter squadrons and two training squadrons with 300 F-14As, and another 24 F-14Cs on order. While these Tomcats are assigned to carriers operating throughout the world, those assigned to the US Navy

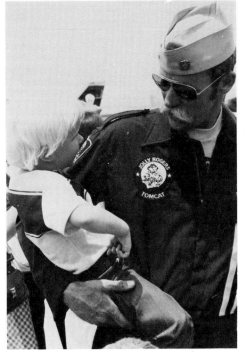

Sixth Fleet in the Mediterranean Sea have seen the most action. These F-14s flew frequent patrols over Lebanon during 1983 and 1984 when the US Marines were stationed there and again in 1985 when a hijacked TransWorld Airlines Boeing 727 and its passengers were being held there.

It was over the Mediterranean that US Navy F-14s had their first taste of live

combat. This incident took place during a US Navy exercise in the international waters of the Gulf of Sidra north of Libya in August 1981. At 7:15 am on the morning of 19 August a pair of Tomcats from VF-41 (the *Black Aces*) aboard the USS *Nimitz* encountered a pair of Libyan Arab Air Force Su-22s (NATO codename 'Fitter'). One of the Soviet-built fighters fired an air-to-air missile at the American planes, which in turn took evasive action. As the two Libyan planes flashed by, the Americans gave chase. The Tomcat flown by Lt Larry Muczynski and Lt James Anderson went after the Fitter who had launched the missile and destroyed it with an AIM-9 Sidewinder missile at a range of about 2600 feet. The other F-14, flown by Commander Hank Kleemann and Lt Dave Venlet easily followed the second Su-22 through a tight turn and shot it down with a Sidewinder.

The Navy pilots used the Sidewinder rather than the Phoenix because the encounter had been a close-in dogfight rather than a long-range interception. They could have destroyed the Libyan aircraft earlier and at greater range with the Phoenix, but they didn't go on the attack until they had been fired upon first. The Gulf of Sidra Incident, as it has come to be known, was the first air-to-air combat involving American pilots flying American jets since the end of the Vietnam War in 1973. It was also the first live combat involving American fourth-generation combat aircraft. Nearly 40 years after the first Wildcats had roared into the sky over the Pacific to do battle with the Japanese Empire's aerial samurai, a Grumman 'cat had tangled with a hostile enemy and had emerged victorious.

US Navy Tomcats went into action over the Mediterranean once again on the moonless night of 10 October 1985, intercepting and forcing down the jetliner carrying the hijackers of the cruise ship *Achille Lauro*, who thought they were in the process of successfully escaping.

On 4 January 1989, in another run-in with the Libyan air force, a pair of Tomcats from the carrier USS *John F Kennedy* were attacked by a pair of MiG-23s (NATO codename Flogger) over the Mediterranean north of Tobruk. In an engagement that lasted just 76 seconds, one MiG was destroyed by an AIM-9 Sidewinder, the other by one of three AIM-7 Sparrows fired at the enemy aircraft. This engagement marked only the second air-to-air combat action experienced by American aircraft since Vietnam, and as with the first, F-14s were two for nought.

THE F-14D/TOMCAT 21 PROGRAMS

In 1986, the Navy began considering an upgrade to the Tomcat fleet, which has gone through a number of permutations, and they have been designated with such nomenclature as F-14A Plus, F-14D and Tomcat 21. These upgrades included better engines and avionics.

Supplanting the Tomcat fleet with the Advanced Tactical Fighter (ATF) being developed for the Air Force was considered an an option in 1986, insisted upon by Congress in 1988 and then tentatively rejected in favor of the F-14D in 1989, when it became clear that a naval ATF (NATF) couldn't be in squadron service until the year 2000.

In the meantime, the Navy went ahead with F-14A Plus, which was an intermediate step toward the F-14D, and which was powered by the General Electric F110 turbofan. The last F-14A was delivered in March 1987 and the first of 38 all new F-14A Plus aircraft was delivered in November 1987, as was the First F-14A equipped with an F-14D avionics package.

The original order for 304 F-14Ds, powered by General Electric 56,000 lb thrust F110-GE-400 turbofans, was trimmed to 127 in March 1987 in favor of

'remanufacturing' 400 F-14As and F-14A Pluses to F-14D standard.

A key part of the F-14D program is the new Hughes AN/APG-71 radar, which offers high speed digital processing, resulting in a sixfold improvement over the F-14A analog system. The new radar introduced monopulse angle tracking and digital scan control. The monopulse technique locates the target precisely within the radar beam. While operating in a track-while-scan mode, digital control of the antenna scan pattern enables the radar to take an occasional scan from target tracking to look for other aircraft. Noncooperative target recognition allows an analysis of the radar return to establish target identification.

The avionics upgrade replaced much of the 1960s-vintage analog avionics with modern digital equipment. The improvements included dual 1553B data bus architecture driven by two US Navy standard AYK-14 mission computers, programmable digital controls and displays, a digital intertial navigation system and a digital stores management system. In addition, an infrared search and rack set was integrated with two existing sensors (radar and television camera set).

First delivered in early 1990, the F-14D utilizes the Joint Tactical Information Distribution System (JTIDS), a secure, jam-resistant data network using a digital transmission technique. Information pro-

Above: Grumman Aerospace proposed its versatile Tomcat 21 concept to the US Navy in 1988, even as the F-14D Tomcat *(right)* was undergoing flight testing. Both types incorporate vastly improved avionics systems.

mulgated by JTIDS can include the position, identity and status of friendly forces; enemy tracks and positions; as well as command data, weather information and digitized voice. In addition, the Airborne Self Protection Jammer (ASPJ) and a new radar warning receiver vastly improves upon the F-14A's current defensive electronic countermeasures capability. The SPJ unit, manufactured by ITT and Westinghouse, is also used by the Air Force. Another facet of the avionics upgrade is an option for integration of the AIM-120 Advanced Medium-Range Air-to-Air Missile (AMRAAM).

The Tomcat 21 proposal, first suggested by Grumman at the end of 1988, involved a further upgrade to the F-14D that included reducing its radar signature, increasing fuel capacity by 2500 pounds and providing it with surface attack capability that included SLAM, Maverick or Harpoon antiship missiles. The Tomcat 21 was seen as a way to give the Navy a serious alternative to the NATF, which it was reluctant to buy, remembering its experience with the TFX, two decades before. For Grumman, it was a way to extend Tomcat production in the face of Congressional efforts to limit F-14D production.

FROM A VENERABLE LINE

Artyem Mikoyan and Mikhail Gur-evich formed the aircraft design bureau (OKB) that bears their name in 1939. After a series of relatively insignificant aircraft during World War II, the team succeeded in developing the Soviet Union's finest first-generation jet fighter, the MiG-15. This aircraft was followed by the similar, though somewhat larger, MiG-17, the supersonic MiG-19 and the ubiquitous MiG-21. Perhaps the most important Soviet warplane since World War II, the MiG-21 first entered Soviet service in 1958 and went on to serve with 33 air forces around the world. With over 10,000 air-craft having been built, the MiG-21 will probably remain in service for more than four decades. By early 1967, the MiG-21 had seen live combat service with India against Pakistan, and North Vietnamese MiG-21s were dueling with US Phantoms over Southeast Asia.

The MiG-23 interceptor, and the similar MiG-27 fighter-bomber which entered service in 1972, had a system of variable geometry wings like the American F-111 and F-14. Used extensively in Afghani-stan by the Soviet air force, these two aircraft—which share the NATO report-ing name Flogger—also have been exported widely to Warsaw Pact and other Soviet sphere countries.

The MiG-25 (NATO codename Foxbat) is a Mach 3 interceptor that was designed in the 1960s to counter the American Mach 3 B-70 bomber. The MiG-25 evolved into the MiG-31 (NATO codename Fox-hound), an outwardly similar interceptor with highly upgraded avionics that was deployed in 1983.

In the meantime, the Mikoyan OKB (the Gurevich name is no longer used, although the abbreviation is still MiG) set about to design a true fourth-generation fighter, an effort which succeeded very well. The MiG-29 (NATO codename Ful-crum) is a twin-engined fighter with a high thrust to weight ratio that is signifi-cantly improved over earlier MiGs. Simi-lar in size and configuration to the

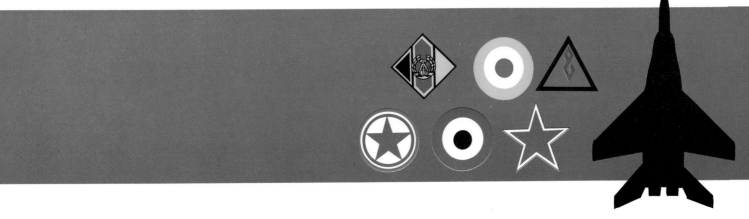

Above: Within the first five years of its service life the MiG-29 was in the inventory of the air forces of East Germany, India, Iraq, North Korea, Syria and the Soviet Union.

Below: This two-seat MiG-29U (*Uti*) was one of two MiG-29s to make an appearance at the Paris Air Show in June 1989.

304

American F/A-18, the MiG-29 is the first Soviet fighter designed with an aerodynamically blended wing fuselage transition.

The MiG-29 was first seen by Western 'observers' at the Ramenskoye test facility in March 1979, and it entered squadron service six years later. It made its first appearance in the West in July 1986 during a visit to Rissala AB in Finland. In September 1988, a MiG-29 and a MiG-29U (*Uti*) trainer made a surprise visit to the Farnborough Air Show in Britain, where they presented an aerobatic display that left the audience very impressed with the aircraft. Included in the demonstration was the tail slide maneuver in which an aircraft climbs vertically, decelerates, stops in midair and slides backward and downward before accelerating. A thrilling maneuver, the tail slide is often performed by piston-engined aircraft, but rarely attempted by jets.

In June 1989, a pair of MiG-29s paid a visit to the Paris Air Show, which was largely a replay of their performance at Farnborough. On 8 June, however, one MiG-29 suffered a flame-out at 580 feet during a low speed pass. Mikoyan chief test pilot Anatoly Kvotchur, who had flown the MiG-29 at Farnborough as well, failed in his attempt to restart the engine, steered away from the crowd, punched the controls on his K-36 ejection seat and ejected with seconds to spare.

Kvotchur survived with minor injuries as the aircraft was swallowed in a ball of flame. However, two months later another pair of MiG-29s were back on the air show

circuit with an appearance at Abottsford, Canada.

THE MiG-29 IN DETAIL

A twin-engined fighter with a positive thrust to weight ratio, the MiG-29 is powered by two Isotov RD-33 turbofans. It is the first high-performance Soviet aircraft to make extensive use of blended contour carbon fiber composite structural components. At seven percent of the total weight, however, it is still much less than its Western contemporaries. The MiG-29's landing gear, like those on its predecssor MiGs, are desgined for operations on rugged landing fields. Its vertical tail surfaces are very reminiscent of those used on the MiG-25 and have been copied for the Sukhoi Su-27.

The cockpit has a limited rear view, but is equipped with a head up display and a pulse-Doppler look-down/shoot-down radar system that is supplemented by a laser rangefinder and an infrared tracking sensor. As one Soviet official pointed out,

the MiG-29 is an offensive, not defensive, aircraft. Optimized for offensive air-to-air combat, the aircraft may be armed with six AA-10 or AA-11 air-to-air missiles located on pylons under each wing. AA-8 and AA-9 missiles can also be carried, and the MiG-29 is fitted with a 30mm cannon.

In a potential ground attack role, the MiG-29 can also carry bombs and various types of unguided aerial rocket pods.

THE MiG-29 IN SERVICE

The Soviet Union operates more than 450 MiG-29s, with those being assigned chiefly to the western Soviet Union, East Germany and Hungary. Also contained in these numbers are perhaps 100 MiG-29U trainers. Export customers include India, Iraq, North Korea, Syria and Yugoslavia. East Germany is the only Warsaw Pact use, and Zimbabwe has been mentioned as a token future recipient.

In the Soviet arsenal, increasing numbers of MiG-29s will be introduced until they have generally replaced the existing Su-15s, MiG-21s and MiG-23s. They will ultimately form the backbone of Soviet tactical air power well into the twenty-first century.

Above: A MiG-29 on long-range patrol, equipped with auxiliary fuel tanks. *Below:* The MiG-29 has a thrust-to-weight ratio of 1.2 or better, facilitating smooth vertical climbs.
Right: Claude Gluntz captured this spectacular photo of Anatoly Kvotchur escaping from his crippled MiG-29 on 8 June 1989, a split second before it exploded.

MIKOYAN-GUREVICH MiG-29

Year first deployed:	1985
Type:	Single-seat air superiority fighter
Power Plant:	Two Isotov RD-33 afterburning turbofans at 18,300 lb thrust
Wingspan:	37 ft 2 in
Length:	56 ft 10 in
Height:	15 ft 6 in
Gross Weight:	39,700 lb
Empty Weight:	18,025 lb
Maximum Speed:	Mach 2 at altitude; 1.1 at sea level
Range:	650 mi; 1300 mi ferry
Service Ceiling:	56,000 ft
Fixed Armament:	One 30mm cannon
Users:	East Germany, India, Iraq, North Korea, Syria, USSR

SUKHOI Su-27

CREAM OF THE CROP

During World War I, the Yakovlev OKB (design bureau) emerged as the principal builder of Soviet fighters. With the advent of jet fighters, however, the Mikoyan-Gurevich OKB superseded Yakovlev in its primacy among fighters. In the late 1950s, as Yakovlev generally moved away from combat aircraft (except for the Yak-38 STOL carrier fighter), Sukhoi replaced it as the Soviet Union's 'second source' for tactical aircraft.

Sukhoi's notable second-generation aircraft included the Su-15 (NATO codename Flagon) interceptor and the Su-7/Su-17 (NATO codename Fitter), a ground attack aircraft.

Appearing on the scene more recently have been the Su-24 (NATO codename Fencer), an outstanding long-range fighter-bomber and the Su-25 (NATO codename Frogfoot), a heavily armed and armored short-range attack aircraft used extensively in Afghanistan between 1984 and 1989.

In 1986, the Soviet air force took delivery of the Su-27 (NATO codename Flanker), which is the best and most advanced fighter ever produced by the Sukhoi OKB, and perhaps in the Soviet Union. Like the MiG-29, the Su-27 is a twin-tailed, twin-engined jet fighter that employs blended contour construction which utilizes carbon fiber components. It is also endowed with pulse-Doppler look-down/shoot-down radar like that of the MiG-29.

First tested in 1977, the Su-27 is now built at Komsomolsk near Khabarovsk. The Su-28 is in the same size and weight class as the McDonnell Douglas F-25 and probably owes something of its design inspiration to the F-15. In service since 1986, the Su-27 was first seen in the West when a pair of them were displayed at the Paris Air Show in June 1989. The Su-27's aerobatic demonstration was as impressive as the debut of the MiG-29 a year earlier at Farnborough, England, and it also included the thrilling tail slide maneuver.

Below: The Sukhoi design bureau's Su-27 is one of the best Soviet warplanes of the 1990s and is, perhaps, the best airplane that Sukhoi ever designed. It was one of the first Soviet planes to incorporate a blended contour fuselage, a feature which assists lift and reduces drag, as well as trimming the aircraft's radar signature.

Above: At the time that this edition was prepared, the Soviet Union was the only nation to have this remarkable fighter in service.

THE Su-27 IN DETAIL

A twin-engined fighter with a positive thrust to weight ratio 1.1:1, the Su-27 is powered by a pair of Lyulka AL-31 turbofans delivering 27,500 lb of thrust. A specially enhanced Su-27, known as P-42, was used to achieve four major time-to-height records, including a climb to 39,370 feet in 55.5 seconds.

The Su-27 is a single seat aircraft, although a small number of nearly identical, combat capable, dual seat Su-27U (*Uti*) training variants have also been produced.

Like the MiG-29, the Su-27 is armed with a 30mm cannon. Its additional armament consists of seven to 10 air-to-air missiles, including AA-8, AA-10 and AA-11 types. Provisions for air-to-ground armament are also present, but this is a decidedly secondary role.

The Su-27 is equipped with the K-36DM ejection seat, similar to that used by Anatoly Kvotchur in his famous 'punch-out' at the 1989 Paris Air Show.

THE Su-27 IN SERVICE

Roughly 100 Su-27s were delivered in the first three years of service, with these being assigned principally to the Legnica and Vinnitsa Air Armies of the Soviet Air Force. Ultimately, they will be used both as interceptors and as long-range escorts for the Su-24. With their long range, both the Su-24 and Su-27 have the capability of reaching targets throughout Western Europe (including Britain) from Warsaw Pact bases. In the interceptor role, the Su-27's look-down/shoot-down radar makes it very effective against low-flying aircraft and cruise missiles.

The Su-27 is also being considered by the Soviet navy for use aboard the latter's first full-size aircraft carrier, which is expected to be in service in the 1990s. The Su-27 itself is expected to become one of the primary fighter aircraft in Soviet service in the 1990s and to remain in this role well into the next century.

SUKHOI Su-27	
Year first deployed:	1986
Type:	Single-seat interceptor, escort fighter
Power Plant:	Two Lyulka AL-31 afterburning turbofans at 27,500 lb thrust
Wingspan:	48 ft 3 in
Length:	70 ft 10.5 in
Gross Weight:	44,000 lb
Maximum Speed:	Mach 2 at altitude; 1.1 at sea level
Range:	930 mi; 1860 mi ferry
Service Ceiling:	60,000 ft
Fixed Armament:	One 30mm cannon
User:	USSR

Above: An Su-27 is towed into position. Note the unpainted metal ahead of the gun port. This Su-27 is otherwise unarmed, in contrast to that pictured *below*, which is equipped with a variation of the AA-2 air-to-air missile.

Right: In this stunning view, the Su-27's similarity to the American F-15 can be seen. Note in particular the intakes and tail surfaces.

Below: As the canopy comes down, this Su-27 pilot prepares to take to the air. Located immediately ahead of the cockpit is the Su-27's search and track radar system. This versatile aircraft is equipped with oversize landing gear and mudflaps to permit operations from crude remote landing strips.

A grid protects the Su-27's Lyulka AL-31F engines from foreign objects. When in flight, the rearward hinged grid slides downward and is held in place by a locking system.

McDONNELL DOUGLAS
F-15 EAGLE

WHERE AIR SUPERIORITY COMES FIRST

The McDonnell Douglas F-15 Eagle may well be the best air-to-air fighter in service in the 1980s. Conceived and designed to be the best possible air-superiority fighter, McDonnell Douglas and the US Air Force spared no expense in its development. If the success with which it was used by the Israeli Air Force in 1982 is any indication, the work put into the Eagle was worthwhile.

To understand the F-15, it is valuable to go back a bit into its family tree. It is part of a line of jet fighters developed in St Louis by the company founded by James Smith McDonnell in 1939, whose first production aircraft, the FH-1 Phantom, was the US Navy's first jet fighter. McDonnell, who believed that inanimate objects had a life of their own, would name all of his fighters after malevolent spirits. The Eagle would be the first exception. After the FH-1 came the F2H Banshee and F3H Demon, which filled the US Navy's inventories during the 1950s. At the same time, McDonnell was building the XF-85 Demon and XF-88 Voodoo experimental aircraft for the US Air Force. Up through the 1950s, McDonnell's most successful aircraft was the F-101 Voodoo, one of the Century series, which represented an advancement of the original XF-88 idea.

The late 1950s saw McDonnell at work on a Navy fighter-bomber that would one day prove to be the best US fighter since the Sabre Jet and the top fighter in not only the US Navy and US Air Force, but the British Royal Air Force and the West German Luftwaffe as well. The Phantom II started life under the US Navy designation F4H, with the US Air Force adopting it as F-110. In 1962 both were redesignated F-4 and the Phantom II went into production. During the war in Southeast Asia, it was the first-line American warplane, racking up thousands of hours as an air-superiority fighter, armed reconnaissance aircraft, and fighter-bomber. Of the 137 North Vietnamese aircraft shot

Top right: Next to the top-view silhouette of the F-15 Eagle are the military insignias of the user nations. From left to right: Israel, Japan, Saudi Arabia and the United States.

Above: A USAF F-15 based at Soesterberg AB, Holland. The F-15 was the first USAF fighter to receive the radar-absorbing pale blue/grey color scheme.

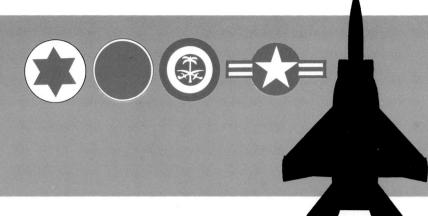

down by the US Air Force during the war, 78 percent were dispatched by Phantoms, while 66 percent of the Navy's air-to-air victories were attributed to Phantoms. By the time the war ended, McDonnell, now a component of McDonnell Douglas, had built over 4300 Phantoms for customers all over the world.

Around the time of the McDonnell Douglas merger in 1967 the US Air Force began to actively think about a successor to the F-4. When the third-generation F-4 was being developed a decade earlier, it was designed for a variety of roles. It was intended to be useful as an interceptor, an air-superiority fighter, or a fighter-bomber. This meant compromise. No plane could be designed to do all three and at the same time be extremely good at any one. While the F-4 did a very good job, better than most, the handwriting was on the wall at the Pentagon.

There were really two major factors that caused the Air Force to change its mind about fighters in the late 1960s. First, there was the evaluation of F-4 performance in Southeast Asia. The Phantom did well in air combat, shooting down 2 enemy aircraft for the loss of a single Phantom, but, while this was good, F-86 Sabre Jets in Korea a generation before had shot down 14 enemy MiGs for the loss of a single Sabre. Part of this had to do with pilot training, part of it with severe restrictions placed on American pilots in Southeast Asia, but part of it was the F-4's being a very complicated airplane designed for a variety of roles.

The second factor was the advent of a new generation of Russian fighters, notably the MiG-25 Foxbat. Flying three times the speed of sound, the Foxbat could fly reconnaissance or strike missions without fear of being intercepted by a missile-armed Phantom.

Above: The precursor to the F-15, the F-4 Phantom.

Right: The F-15D, the two-seat trainer version of the F-15C, prior to delivery to the USAF.

In December 1967, the Air Force awarded concept-formulation-study contracts to General Dynamics and McDonnell Douglas for a high-performance, all-weather, single-seat jet fighter, with a high thrust-to-weight ratio that was capable of speeds up to Mach 2.5, under a program called FX (Fighter, Experimental). Two years later, on 31 December 1969, the Air Force signed a developmental contract with McDonnell Douglas for the new fighter under the designation YF-15. The plane rolled out of the St Louis factory on 26 June 1972, at which time it was christened Eagle. The first flight, at the hands of McDonnell chief test pilot Irv Burrows, took place at Edwards AFB on 17 July lasting nearly an hour and demonstrating the Eagle's potential. The production go-ahead came in February 1973, with the first deliveries coming in November 1974.

In January 1975 the nineteenth F-15 was stripped down for the purpose of breaking

a number of world speed records and re-christened 'Streak Eagle.' In just over two weeks of flying out of Grand Forks AFB, North Dakota, the 'Streak Eagle' broke eight time-to-altitude records, three of them held by the notorious MiG-25 Foxbat, and in doing so demonstrated the F-15's ability to accelerate to supersonic speeds while climbing straight up. The margins by which the Streak Eagle shattered existing records ranged from 15 percent to 33 percent, with the latter being a climb to 49,212 feet (15,000 meters) in 77 seconds, compared to almost two minutes taken by the previous record holder, an F-4 Phantom.

Below: The Number One F-15 in the final stages of assembly at McDonnell Douglas in 1972 *(left)* compared with a USAF 36th TFW F-15C from Bitburg AB, Germany, photographed 10 years later *(right).*

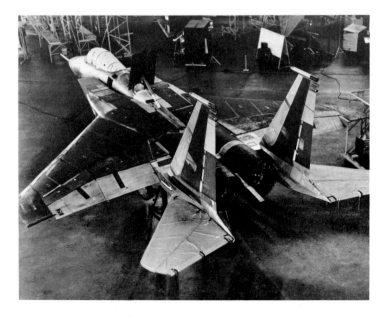

THE EAGLE IN DETAIL

The Eagle, for all its speed and power, is designed to be an easy plane to fly. It is a highly automated weapons system that a pilot can fly instinctively. Perched high in his bubble canopy, the pilot has a 360 degree field of vision, and need not even look down at his instrument panel because all the data he needs, such as speed, altitude, target range, etc, are projected onto the canopy by a system called a Head-Up Display (HUD). Fighter pilots love the Eagle because it is designed to serve its pilots, not vice-versa. While the F-4 Phantom, like many planes of its era, had been developed under the 'multirole' theory, the Eagle was designed as a fighter, a 'fighter pilot's fighter.'

The Eagle's talons consist of much of the same armament proven aboard the F-4, and more. The 20mm multibarreled cannon is there, as is the provision for four AIM-7 Sparrow air-to-air missiles, semi-recessed into the fuselage. Underwing pylons can accommodate other types of stores, ranging from AIM-9 Sidewinder missiles, to bombs, to electronic counter measures (ECM) pods. The Eagle's offensive avionics systems are designed to easily accommodate new missiles and weapons that may be developed, such as the AIM-120 Advanced Medium Range

McDONNELL DOUGLAS F-15 EAGLE

	F-15A*	F-15C*
Year first deployed:	1976	1979
Type:	Single-seat air-superiority fighter	Single-seat fighter
Power Plant:	Two Pratt & Whitney F100-PW-100 turbofans @ 23,820 lb thrust each w/afterburners	Two Pratt & Whitney F100-PW-100 afterburning turbofans @ 23,930 lb thrust each
Wingspan:	42 ft 10 in	42 ft 10 ft
Length:	63 ft 9 in	63 ft 9 in
Height:	18 ft 5 in	18 ft 5 in
Wing Area:	608 sq ft	608 sq ft
Gross Weight:	41,500 lb	68,000 lb
Empty Weight:	28,000 lb	28,000 lb
Maximum Speed:	Mach 2.5 @ altitude; Mach 1.2 @ sea level	Mach 2.5 @ altitude; Mach 1.2 @ sea level
Range:	2400 mi ferry	3400 mi ferry w/external tanks
Service Ceiling:	65,000 ft	65,000 ft
Fixed Armament:	One General Electric M61 20mm Vulcan	One General Electric 20mm M61 cannon
Users:	Israel, Japan, Saudi Arabia, USAF	Israel, Japan, USAF
	*The F-15B is the two-seat trainer version of the F-15A	*The F-15D is the two-seat trainer version of the F-15C. The F-15E is the two-seat strike version of the F-15D.

Left: F-15Ds with AIM-7 Sparrow AAMs under the fuselage and AIM-9 Sidewinders under the wings.

Bottom left: The HUD, perched at eye-level, instantly provides the F-15 pilot with instrument readings.

Below: A cutaway rendering the internal structure of a single-seat F-15. The pink areas are fuel tanks and fuel lines.

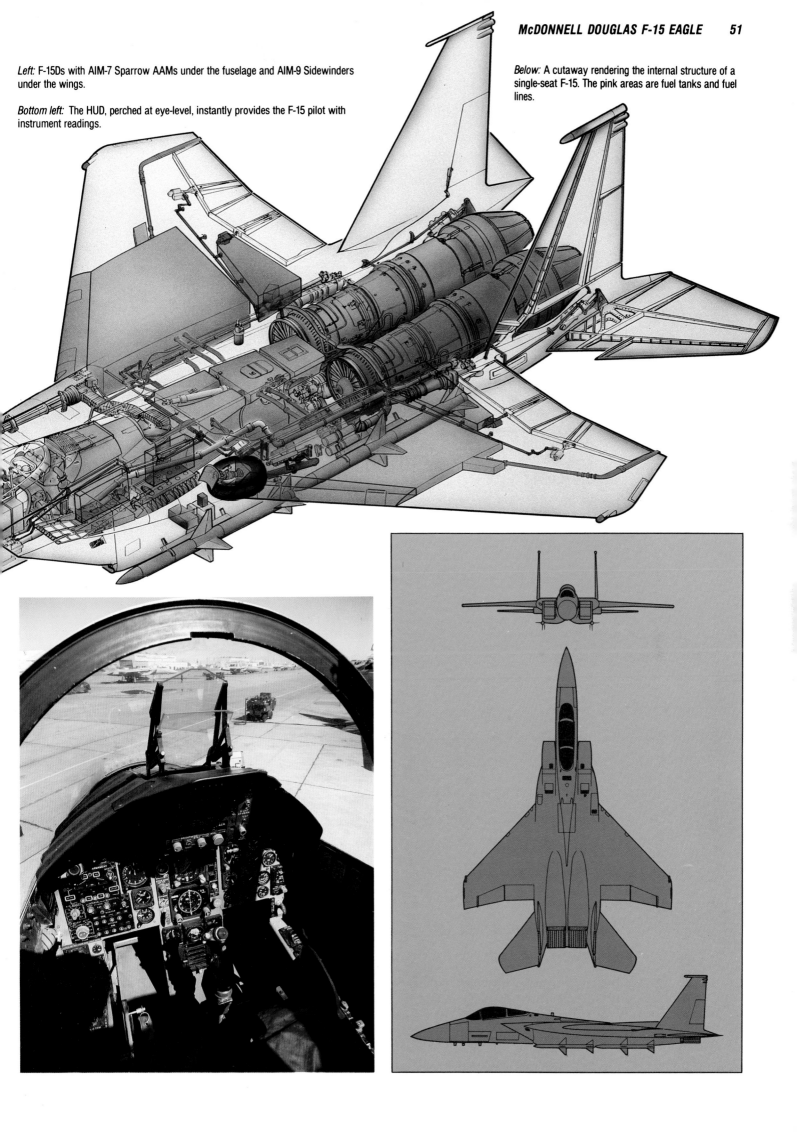

Above: F-15 ground crew personnel at Langley AFB.

Top left: An F-15 successfully tested the booster system of the ASAT missile in September 1985.

Two Middle Eastern air forces operate F-15s: Israel *(right)* and Saudi Arabia *(left).*

Air-to-Air Missile (AMRAAM). In January 1984, an F-15 successfully test fired the Air Launched Miniature Vehicle (ALMV) two-stage, anti-satellite (ASAT) missile.

The F-15 is powered by two Pratt & Whitney F100 turbo fans, delivering an aggregate of 47,640 lb of thrust, more than 33 percent than that available to the F-4E, which has a gross weight six tons heavier than that of the F-15.

THE EAGLE IN SERVICE

The first US Air Force unit to become fully operational with the Eagle was the First Tactical Fighter Wing at Langley AFB (Tactical Air Command Headquarters) in January 1976. The first overseas deployment of USAF Eagles was to Bitburg AB in Germany later the same year. The initial deliveries consisted primarily of the F-15A, but these were complimented by a small number of fully combat-capable F-15B two-seat trainers. By the end of September 1977 there had been deliveries of 245 F-15s to the Air Force, and by April 1980 the total had more than doubled to 504. Eagles were assigned to both training and operational bases in the United States, as well as overseas to Germany and to Kadena AB on Okinawa. In January 1979, 12 F-15s were temporarily deployed to Khmis Mishayt RSAFB in Saudi Arabia at

the request of the Saudi government, who had, coincidentally, placed an order for 60 F-15s of their own.

In June 1969 the second series of Eagles made their appearance under the designations F-15C and F-15D, with the F-15D being the two-seat trainer version of the F-15C. Outwardly identical to the F-15A/B, the new Eagles had greatly upgraded avionics, centerline FAST (Fuel And Sensor, Tactical) Pack drop tanks, additional internal fuel capacity, and structural enhancement to permit heavier loads. Under the 1983 Multi-Stage Improvement Program (MSIP II), even more upgrading is being introduced into the F-15C/D program. Under MSIP II, (MSIP I would upgrade existing F-15A/Bs) the Eagles' weapons systems are being improved and their APG-63 radar is having its memory increased from 96K to 1000K. It will now be possible for the APG-63 to process information at a rate of 1.4 million operations per second, three times faster than before. The plane's central computer, meanwhile, will be able to store four times the data and process it three times as fast. The Armament Control System control panel in the cockpit is being replaced by a multipurpose color video screen. Meanwhile, an equally potent, though less sophisticated, unofficial addition has been a six-power rifle scope adjacent to the HUD on the plane's

centerline. This has greatly aided in the identification of opposing aircraft in simulated air combat exercises.

The first foreign deliveries of F-15s were the sale of 8 to Japan under the Peace Eagle I program. This was followed by the sales to Israel under the Peace Fox program, and to Saudi Arabia under Peace Sun. An additional 4 McDonnell-built F-15s were delivered to Japan in 1983, where 86 Eagles are being built by Mitsubishi under the designation F-15J.

The Eagle's first taste of combat came in June, 1979, when six Israeli F-15s and two Kfirs were jumped by approximately the same number of MiG-21s. Within three minutes, six of the attackers had been shot down, five of them by F-15s. On September 24 of the same year, Israeli F-15s engaged four more MiG-21s, shooting them all down without a loss to their own number.

In June 1982 Syria moved mobile SA-6 surface-to-air missile (SAM) launchers into the Bakaa Valley to intimidate Israeli Air Force (IAF) reconnaissance flights over Lebanon. When Israeli aircraft attacked the SA-6 sites, they were in turn attacked by Russian-built MiGs with Syrian markings, which were presumably flown by Syrian pilots. Two major air battles and several small skirmishes during the first week of June resulted in the MiGs facing off against American-built F-15s and F-16s. By the end of the week, 55 MiGs had been shot down without the loss of a single Israeli fighter. Because the IAF only recognizes kills that can be proven by gun-camera footage, the total may actually have been higher. An Israeli A-4 Skyhawk attack plane had been shot down, but by a SAM and not a Syrian

fighter. At the end of a month of air-to-air combat over Lebanon, 81 Syrian fighters had been downed, with no losses recorded on the Israeli side. Of the total victories, 60 percent are credited to the F-15, with at least three of these kills coming in combat with the sinister MiG-25 Foxbat.

Even if the Israelis had lost an Eagle to the Syrians, the kill ratio for the F-15 still would have been *28 times* better than the F-4 in Vietnam and four times better than the F-86 in Korea. Some of this probably has to do with circumstance and with training (Israeli as well as American fighter pilots of the 1980s are far better trained for air combat than USAF pilots of the 1960s), but a lot has to do with the Eagle.

During 1983, US Air Force F-15s were sent to the Sudan to counter a possible threat by Libya, but they deployed back to their bases, having perhaps caused Libyan dictator Quaddafi to think twice. In June 1984, Saudi Arabia became the second nation whose Eagles were involved in air combat. The war between Iran and Iraq, then in its fourth year of bloody stalemate, spilled over into the Persian Gulf when Iranian aircraft began bombing oil tankers in international waters. A pair of Saudi F-15s intercepted one of these aircraft, ironically a McDonnell Douglas Phantom, and blew it out of the sky.

Though they developed the Eagle *strictly* as an air-superiority fighter, the people of McDonnell Douglas continued to keep alive the notion of the F-15's potential as a fighter-bomber. The potential was originally demonstrated in the 1970s with a specially prepared bomb-carrying F-15 they called the 'Strike Eagle.' The Strike Eagle idea was still alive and well in the St Louis headquarters of McDonnell Douglas in 1983 when the

Top: An F-15C of the US Air Force Fourth Tactical Fighter Wing lights its afterburner for a supersonic dash.

Above: An Eagle driver confers with a member of his crew. The image of the Eagle as hunter has been accentuated by the use of hunting rifle scopes that some pilots have mounted to the right of the HUD.

Below right: The first F-15E Strike Eagle was flown in 1986, and by 1988 service deliveries of production Strike Eagles *(right)* had begun. The F-15E is equipped with LANTIRN for all-weather operations and carries a wide assortment of ordnance.

USAF Tactical Air Command went looking for a dual-role fighter/fighter-bomber to replace its aging fleet of F-111s in the long-range, deep-interdiction mission. The Air Force compared the Strike Eagle, now known at McDonnell as the Dual Role Fighter Demonstrator (DRFD), to General Dynamics' F-16XL, a delta-winged, bomb-carrying development of their F-16 Fighting Falcon fighter.

On 24 February 1984, Chief of Staff General Charles Gabriel announced that the USAF had picked the DRFD and would spend $1.5 billion to procure them as fighter-bombers under the designation F-15E. The first F-15E was flown on 11 December 1986.

The F-15E is essentially a modified F-15D with 96 percent of its systems in common with other Eagles. The two-man cockpit is equipped with Hughes APG-70 radar and is modified to accommodate a weapons system operator in the back seat. The F-15E is capable of carrying bomb loads of up to 23 tons, including nuclear weapons, with a gross weight 19 percent greater than an F-15C. It can also carry air-to-air missiles and convert to the air-superiority role. Powered by a pair of Pratt & Whitney F100-220 turbofans, the F-15E can carry such air-to-ground ordnance as GBU-12 and GBU-15 glide bombs and AGM-65 Maverick missiles. By 1989, 123 of the 392 F-15s had been delivered.

On 7 September 1988, McDonnell Douglas began testing an F-15 Short Take-off and Landing (STOL) demonstrator. The

aircraft was equipped with canards and vectorable jet nozzles. Demonstrations have shown that the aircraft can take off in 1500 feet with a three-ton payload—one-third the distance needed by an F-15B— and land in 1250 feet on a wet runway. STOL characteristics are seen as essential to adapting aircraft to operations from damaged runways during wartime conditions. A STOL F-15 will not be produced, but rather the demonstrator will help in the development of future aircraft types.

By 1989 the US Air Force, the principal user of the F-15, had a total of 718 Eagles in active service, with another 99 assigned to the Air National Guard. Deliveries will continue to the mid-1990s, for a total of 1266 aircraft.

PANAVIA
TORNADO

EUROPE'S LEADING MULTINATIONAL COMBAT AIRCRAFT PROGRAM

The Tornado is important in our consideration of modern combat aircraft for several reasons. It is the first major first-echelon combat aircraft to be developed jointly by three different manufacturers in three different countries. Furthermore, it is the leading combat aircraft in each of the three nations where it is produced and operated.

The idea for a high-performance, international cooperative aircraft that led ultimately to the Tornado goes back to the 1960s. The British had been exploring such a joint venture with the French, as had the Germans and the Americans. When these deals fell through, the British and the Germans joined forces on the project. The Canadian, Belgian, Dutch and Italian governments also expressed interest, but only the Italians stayed in.

As a result, Panavia GmbH was formed in 1969 in Munich, West Germany, for the express purpose of developing a Multirole Combat Aircraft (MRCA). Panavia, a tri-national consortium containing British Aerospace, Italy's Aeritalia, and Germany's Messerschmitt-Bölkow-Blohm (MBB), would develop the total system and build the airframe. The engines, meanwhile, would be built by another tri-national consortium set up expressly for the project. The engine manufacturer, Turbo-Union, was composed of Fiat in Italy, Motoren & Turbinen Union (MTU) in Germany, and Britain's leading jet engine builder, Rolls-Royce. Joint ventures such as the Tornado program offer lower development costs to each participating nation than do purely national programs, while at the same time permitting the companies to remain competitive in state-of-the-art technology through the sharing of research, development and production investment costs.

The firms represented in the Panavia consortium bring to the Tornado a family tree that includes some of Europe's best. British Aerospace is itself the consortium into which were funneled all of Britain's most famous military aircraft builders

from Hawker to Avro. Aeritalia is yet another consortium whose backbone was Fiat, the industrial giant among whose products was the G91 series, Italy's first major postwar combat aircraft. Messerschmitt-Bölkow-Blohm, a consortium of three German firms, was in large measure the legacy of Professor Willy Messerschmitt, whose aircraft had been a major factor in Germany's Luftwaffe during World War II. His Bf-109, produced in larger numbers than any other fighter in history, was one of the war's top aircraft, and his Me-262 was the world's first operational jet fighter. Professor Messerschmitt, who died in 1971, lived just long enough to see production begin on the Tornado.

Production of the Tornado airframe is divided among the three Panavia part-

ners. Aeritalia is primarily responsible for all Tornado wings, MBB for the center fuselage, and British Aerospace for the front and rear fuselage. Final assembly lines are maintained by all three companies at Torino, Italy, Manching, West Germany, and at Warton in the United Kingdom.

Production began on the first prototypes in November 1970, with the first flight of the number 01 prototype taking place at MBB's Manching test field in August 1974. The Tornado made its first public appearance at the Hanover Air Show in April 1976, and the first series production began in July of the same year. In 1978, the RAF base at Cottsmore, South Leicestershire, was assigned to host the Tri-national Tornado Training Establishment (TTTE), where pilots from all three nations would learn to fly the Tornado. The first two Tornados were delivered to the RAF at Cottsmore on 1 July 1980 and three Luftwaffe Tornados arrived on the 2nd and 3rd of September. By 5 January 1981 there were 15 Tornados on hand for the start of the first 13-week training course. At its peak the TTTE can accommodate 135 to 160 crews.

As a Multirole Combat Aircraft, the Tornado was designed for a variety of tactical combat duties. These centered around air-superiority and the Interdictor Strike (IDS) role, but also included tactical reconnaissance. A specialized version, the Air Defence Variant (ADV), has been ordered by Britain's Royal Air Force for use as an interceptor. The two versions of the Tornado, IDS and ADV, are

Below and opposite below: Panavia Tornados on the final assembly line at the MBB plant in Manching, and the first Tornado prototype, also at Manching.

Left and right: The first four services to receive the Tornado were the German, British and Italian air forces and the German Marineflieger.

The British Aerospace prototypes of the two RAF Tornados: the IDS *(above)* and ADV *(far right)*.

Right: The first Luftwaffe instructor crew.

Above right: Tornados of the German Weapon Conversion Unit low over Upper Bavaria.

90 percent similar, with the differences being in the area of radar, avionics, software and weapons systems. Of the 809 Tornados contracted for, 165 ADVs will be delivered to the RAF. The balance will be of the IDS type, with 220 going to the RAF, 212 to the German Luftwaffe, 112 to the German Marineflieger (naval air arm), and 100 to the Italian air force. The Tornado is quantitatively, and probably qualitatively, the most important West European warplane program since World War II.

THE TORNADO IN DETAIL

The nose of the Tornado contains a double-hinged avionics compartment which is home to the plane's radar and avionics hardware. Immediately aft of this compartment is the two-place cockpit containing the pilot and navigator stations under a one-piece canopy. Below the cockpit, two 27mm Mauser cannons are situated on either side of the nose wheel well.

The Tornado has shoulder-mounted variable-geometry wings whose sweep

Left: Easy maintenance and rapid engine changes can be performed on the Tornado with minimum manpower. The metal plates that fold over the top and bottom of the engine are thrust reversers.

can be altered from a nearly straight 25 degrees in their forward position to an acutely swept 67 degrees for high-speed operations. Two pylons are located under each wing for the carrying of auxiliary fuel tanks or offensive weapons. These pylons are designed to swivel as the geometry of the wings is altered, to keep the stores parallel to the fuselage. The torsion box where the two wings meet within the fuselage doubles as an integral fuel tank.

Over half of the aircraft's integral fuel is carried in self-sealing bag tanks in the center fuselage. The MBB-produced center fuselage also contains the auxiliary power unit (APU) which permits the aircraft to be started at remote airfields without complete facilities. In fact, only fuel and ammunition are required to operate the aircraft from dispersed bases. The flat underside of the center fuselage has three parallel pylons for the attachment of fuel tanks or weapons.

The rear fuselage contains a pair of three-spool, reheated Turbo-Union RB-199 turbofan engines separated from each other by a titanium firewall. The engines are electronically controlled and equipped with integral thrust reversers that can be deployed in less than one second.

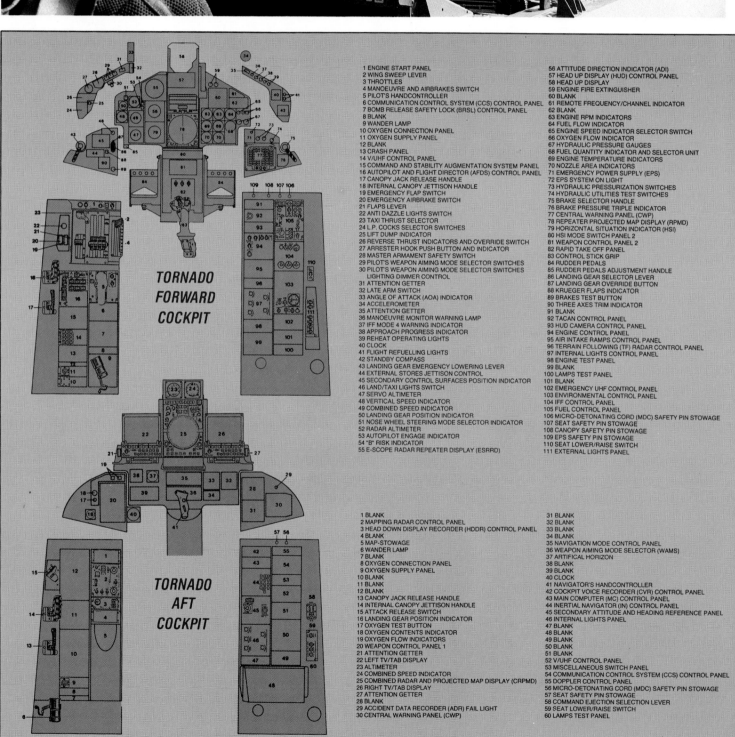

TORNADO
FORWARD
COCKPIT

1 ENGINE START PANEL
2 WING SWEEP LEVER
3 THROTTLES
4 MANOEUVRE AND AIRBRAKES SWITCH
5 PILOT'S HANDCONTROLLER
6 COMMUNICATION CONTROL SYSTEM (CCS) CONTROL PANEL
7 BOMB RELEASE SAFETY LOCK (BRSL) CONTROL PANEL
8 BLANK
9 WANDER LAMP
10 OXYGEN CONNECTION PANEL
11 OXYGEN SUPPLY PANEL
12 BLANK
13 CRASH PANEL
14 V/UHF CONTROL PANEL
15 COMMAND AND STABILITY AUGMENTATION SYSTEM PANEL
16 AUTOPILOT AND FLIGHT DIRECTOR (AFDS) CONTROL PANEL
17 CANOPY JACK RELEASE HANDLE
18 INTERNAL CANOPY JETTISON HANDLE
19 EMERGENCY FLAP SWITCH
20 EMERGENCY AIRBRAKE SWITCH
21 FLAPS LEVER
22 ANTI DAZZLE LIGHTS SWITCH
23 TAXI THRUST SELECTOR
24 L.P. COCKS SELECTOR SWITCHES
25 LIFT DUMP INDICATOR
26 REVERSE THRUST INDICATORS AND OVERRIDE SWITCH
27 ARRESTER HOOK PUSH BUTTON AND INDICATOR
28 MASTER ARMAMENT SAFETY SWITCH
29 PILOT'S WEAPON AIMING MODE SELECTOR SWITCHES
30 PILOT'S WEAPON AIMING MODE SELECTOR SWITCHES
   LIGHTING DIMMER CONTROL
31 ATTENTION GETTER
32 LATE ARM SWITCH
33 ANGLE OF ATTACK (AOA) INDICATOR
34 ACCELEROMETER
35 ATTENTION GETTER
36 MANOEUVRE MONITOR WARNING LAMP
37 IFF MODE 4 WARNING INDICATOR
38 APPROACH PROGRESS INDICATOR
39 REHEAT OPERATING LIGHTS
40 CLOCK
41 FLIGHT REFUELLING LIGHTS
42 STANDBY COMPASS
43 LANDING GEAR EMERGENCY LOWERING LEVER
44 EXTERNAL STORES JETTISON CONTROL
45 SECONDARY CONTROL SURFACES POSITION INDICATOR
46 LAND/TAXI LIGHTS SWITCH
47 SERVO ALTIMETER
48 VERTICAL SPEED INDICATOR
49 COMBINED SPEED INDICATOR
50 LANDING GEAR POSITION INDICATOR
51 NOSE WHEEL STEERING MODE SELECTOR INDICATOR
52 RADAR ALTIMETER
53 AUTOPILOT ENGAGE INDICATOR
54 "B" RISK INDICATOR
55 E-SCOPE RADAR REPEATER DISPLAY (ESRRD)

56 ATTITUDE DIRECTION INDICATOR (ADI)
57 HEAD UP DISPLAY (HUD) CONTROL PANEL
58 HEAD UP DISPLAY
59 ENGINE FIRE EXTINGUISHER
60 BLANK
61 REMOTE FREQUENCY/CHANNEL INDICATOR
62 BLANK
63 ENGINE RPM INDICATORS
64 FUEL FLOW INDICATOR
65 ENGINE SPEED INDICATOR SELECTOR SWITCH
66 OXYGEN FLOW INDICATOR
67 HYDRAULIC PRESSURE GAUGES
68 FUEL QUANTITY INDICATOR AND SELECTOR UNIT
69 ENGINE TEMPERATURE INDICATORS
70 NOZZLE AREA INDICATORS
71 EMERGENCY POWER SUPPLY (EPS)
72 EPS SYSTEM ON LIGHT
73 HYDRAULIC PRESSURIZATION SWITCHES
74 HYDRAULIC UTILITIES TEST SWITCHES
75 BRAKE SELECTOR HANDLE
76 BRAKE PRESSURE TRIPLE INDICATOR
77 CENTRAL WARNING PANEL (CWP)
78 REPEATER PROJECTED MAP DISPLAY (RPMD)
79 HORIZONTAL SITUATION INDICATOR (HSI)
80 HSI MODE SWITCH PANEL 2
81 WEAPON CONTROL PANEL 2
82 RAPID TAKE OFF PANEL
83 CONTROL STICK GRIP
84 RUDDER PEDALS
85 RUDDER PEDALS ADJUSTMENT HANDLE
86 LANDING GEAR SELECTOR LEVER
87 LANDING GEAR OVERRIDE BUTTON
88 KRUEGER FLAPS INDICATOR
89 BRAKES TEST BUTTON
90 THREE AXES TRIM INDICATOR
91 BLANK
92 TACAN CONTROL PANEL
93 HUD CAMERA CONTROL PANEL
94 ENGINE CONTROL PANEL
95 AIR INTAKE RAMPS CONTROL PANEL
96 TERRAIN FOLLOWING (TF) RADAR CONTROL PANEL
97 INTERNAL LIGHTS CONTROL PANEL
98 ENGINE TEST PANEL
99 BLANK
100 LAMPS TEST PANEL
101 BLANK
102 EMERGENCY UHF CONTROL PANEL
103 ENVIRONMENTAL CONTROL PANEL
104 IFF CONTROL PANEL
105 FUEL CONTROL PANEL
106 MICRO-DETONATING CORD (MDC) SAFETY PIN STOWAGE
107 SEAT SAFETY PIN STOWAGE
108 CANOPY SAFETY PIN STOWAGE
109 EPS SAFETY PIN STOWAGE
110 SEAT LOWER/RAISE SWITCH
111 EXTERNAL LIGHTS PANEL

TORNADO
AFT
COCKPIT

1 BLANK
2 MAPPING RADAR CONTROL PANEL
3 HEAD DOWN DISPLAY RECORDER (HDDR) CONTROL PANEL
4 BLANK
5 MAP-STOWAGE
6 WANDER LAMP
7 BLANK
8 OXYGEN CONNECTION PANEL
9 OXYGEN SUPPLY PANEL
10 BLANK
11 BLANK
12 BLANK
13 CANOPY JACK RELEASE HANDLE
14 INTERNAL CANOPY JETTISON HANDLE
15 ATTACK RELEASE SWITCH
16 LANDING GEAR POSITION INDICATOR
17 OXYGEN TEST BUTTON
18 OXYGEN CONTENTS INDICATOR
19 OXYGEN FLOW INDICATORS
20 WEAPON CONTROL PANEL 1
21 ATTENTION GETTER
22 LEFT TV/TAB DISPLAY
23 ALTIMETER
24 COMBINED SPEED INDICATOR
25 COMBINED RADAR AND PROJECTED MAP DISPLAY (CRPMD)
26 RIGHT TV/TAB DISPLAY
27 ATTENTION GETTER
28 BLANK
29 ACCIDENT DATA RECORDER (ADR) FAIL LIGHT
30 CENTRAL WARNING PANEL (CWP)

31 BLANK
32 BLANK
33 BLANK
34 BLANK
35 NAVIGATION MODE CONTROL PANEL
36 WEAPON AIMING MODE SELECTOR (WAMS)
37 ARTIFICAL HORIZON
38 BLANK
39 BLANK
40 CLOCK
41 NAVIGATOR'S HANDCONTROLLER
42 COCKPIT VOICE RECORDER (CVR) CONTROL PANEL
43 MAIN COMPUTER (MC) CONTROL PANEL
44 INERTIAL NAVIGATOR (IN) CONTROL PANEL
45 SECONDARY ATTITUDE AND HEADING REFERENCE PANEL
46 INTERNAL LIGHTS PANEL
47 BLANK
48 BLANK
49 BLANK
50 BLANK
51 BLANK
52 V/UHF CONTROL PANEL
53 MISCELLANEOUS SWITCH PANEL
54 COMMUNICATION CONTROL SYSTEM (CCS) CONTROL PANEL
55 DOPPLER CONTROL PANEL
56 MICRO-DETONATING CORD (MDC) SAFETY PIN STOWAGE
57 SEAT SAFETY PIN STOWAGE
58 COMMAND EJECTION SELECTION LEVER
59 SEAT LOWER/RAISE SWITCH
60 LAMPS TEST PANEL

While the Tornado could be operated on most missions by one person, the two-man crew allows for optimum task sharing as would be required in the complexity of a confused battlefield in foul weather. The pilot sits in the forward station and is charged with flying the aircraft, monitoring systems, visual target acquisition, and air-to-air combat. The navigator, meanwhile, concentrates on mission planning, navigation updating, management of air-to-ground weapons, and acquisition of targets beyond visual range. Both stations are equipped with Martin Baker MK-10A fully automatic, rocket-assisted ejection seats which can be used from 50,000 feet down to ground level, and at speeds up to Mach 2.

The Tornado avionics are controlled by a 64K digital main computer handling navigation, flight direction and terrain following, weapon aiming and delivery, computing, communication, and defense. These subsystems are in turn interlinked with a number of important sensors, including the Ground Mapping Radar (GMR), which allows for low-level navigation in low visibility. The all-weather Terrain-Following Radar (TFR) is one of the most important aids to high-speed,

Opposite: A view of the Tornado's Tactical Navigator's instruments, including a combined radar/moving map display in the center.

Below right: A pre-series Tornado carrying two ECMs, two Kormorans and two Sidewinders.

low-level operations. The terrain data is fed to the flying controls via the auto pilot or shown to the pilot on his Head-Up Display (HUD). The terrain-following system controls the flight path of the aircraft to a preset clearance altitude. The TFR scans the terrain profile, in conditions of both full and zero visibility, and if a hill or other terrain feature appears in the flight path, it tells the autopilot to pull up. The system can be set between 200 and 1500 feet, and is capable of functioning at the Tornado's highest low-level speed. When flying bombing or attack missions against well-defended targets, the need for a reliable, low-level capability is essential.

For its variety of roles, the Tornado carries a variety of weapons in addition to

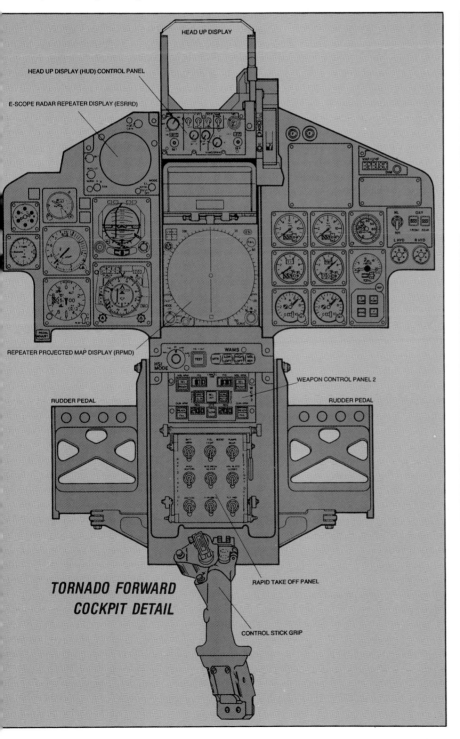

TORNADO FORWARD COCKPIT DETAIL

HEAD UP DISPLAY
HEAD UP DISPLAY (HUD) CONTROL PANEL
E-SCOPE RADAR REPEATER DISPLAY (ESRRD)
REPEATER PROJECTED MAP DISPLAY (RPMD)
RUDDER PEDAL
WAMS
WEAPON CONTROL PANEL 2
RUDDER PEDAL
RAPID TAKE OFF PANEL
CONTROL STICK GRIP

PANAVIA TORNADO

Year first deployed:	1980
Type:	Two-seat multipurpose combat aircraft
Power Plant:	Two Turbo-Union RB.199-34R afterburning turbofans @ 15,000 lb thrust each
Wingspan:	45 ft 7 in spread; 28 ft 2 in swept
Length:	54 ft 9.5 in
Height:	18 ft 8.5 in
Gross Weight:	60,000 lb
Empty Weight:	25,000 lb
Maximum Speed:	Mach 2.2 @ altitude Mach 1.2 @ sea level
Range:	870 mi w/heavy load
Service Ceiling:	50,000 ft
Fixed Armament:	Two Mauser 27mm cannons
Users:	Italy, Oman, Saudi Arabia, United Kingdom, West Germany

its fixed armament of two 27mm Mauser cannons. These weapons can include all standard high explosive bombs, as well as the BL 755 cluster bomb. Area and airfield-denial weapons are the principal armament on interdiction missions. These include the RAF JP-233, which ejects munitions designed to effectively crater runways and delay their repair, as well as the Luftwaffe's MW-1 containers, which can be used with antirunway or antiarmor submunition. Typical air-to-surface guided weapons include GBU-15 TV-guided, or PAVEWAY laser-guided 'smart bombs,' and Maverick guided missiles.

The German *Marineflieger* equips its Tornados with the MBB Kormoran sea-

Above: A Luftwaffe Tornado carrying the MW-1 pod that side fires hundreds of submunitions.

Below: A Luftwaffe Tornado with Marineflieger armament, including four Kormorans, two AIM-9 Sidewinders, ECMs and chaffe/flare dispensers.

Opposite: An RAF Tornado IDS carrying seven Alarm missiles, two fuel tanks and an ECM pod.

skimming, antiship missile, while the RAF uses the BAe Sea Eagle ASM for similar missions. For air-to-air operations, all Tornados are equipped to carry the AIM-9 Sidewinder heat-seeking missile, while the Tornado ADV also carries four Skyflash medium-range missiles as standard equipment.

THE TORNADO IN SERVICE

The first IDS Tornados went into squadron service with the Luftwaffe and the RAF in 1982, with the first RAF Tornados joining 617 Squadron, the 'Dambusters,' of World War II fame. By the end of 1984, the RAF had just over 80 Tornados in service, with six strike squadrons and the first ADVs reporting for duty. The Luftwaffe had, by the end of 1984, 60 Tornados in service, with four *Jagdbombergeschwader* (fighter-bomber wings), these being JaboG 31 ('Boelcke'), JaboG 32, JaboG 33 and JaboG 34. The *Marineflieger*, meanwhile, had 47 Tornados in *Marinefliegergeschwader* (naval air wings), numbers 1 and 2 in Schleswig. The Italian air force, *Reggia Aeronautica*, by this time had 36 Tornados equipping two fighter-bomber recon squadrons.

In August 1985 the Sultanate of Oman became the first nation other than the original Panavia partners to take an active interest in the Tornado, with an order for eight of the Air Defence Variant.

In September 1985 Saudi Arabia ended a year of speculation as it joined Oman and became the second Middle East nation to express an interest in acquiring the Tornado. British Defence Minister

Michael Haseltine and Saudi Defense Minister Sultann Ibn Abdel Aziz reached an agreement whereby the Saudi air force would receive 48 Tornados along with the 30 British Aerospace Hawk trainers in a complicated deal involving British acceptance of Saudi oil as a large part of the payment. It was understood that should the Saudis want early delivery of their Tornados, the British would give up some of the in-production aircraft that were earmarked for them and make it up with later production. The net result in either case would be that the Tornado production line would stay open well into the 1990s.

The typical mission for the Tornado IDS is similar to that for the USAF General Dynamics F-111 and FB-111, which were introduced more than a decade earlier. This mission is to fly the full spectrum of tactical air missions against a massive Warsaw Pact invasion at a moment's notice, and in any kind of weather. Because foul weather is the rule rather

than the exception in Europe, and because mid-winter nights can run to 17 hours of darkness, an all-weather capability is vital. Until the advent of the Tornado, the F-111 was the only aircraft in the NATO arsenal capable of flying interdiction missions with conventional weapons at terrain-hugging altitudes in low or zero visibility. It is now possible to supplement the F-111s with a larger number of more up-to-date, higher-performance Tornados, thus making potential Warsaw Pact operations in Western Europe more difficult and costly.

The need for the RAF's Tornado ADV (Tornado F2 in service) becomes clear when one considers the vastness of the UK Air Defence Region, which stretches from Iceland to the English Channel, and from the British Isles east to Norway. The potential threats include the Soviet Bear long-range bombers that even now routinely fly through the Greenland/Iceland/UK gap, as well as Soviet Backfire bombers and Fencer fighter-bombers that may

Above: A production RAF Tornado ADV in pale grey camouflage, with low-visibility insignia, carrying four Sky Flash missiles, two Sidewinders and two long-range fuel tanks.

Opposite: Two RAF GR Mk1s, each with four 1000 lb bombs, two full fuel tanks and two ECM pods.

attempt to attack Britain, British shipping, or Britain's North Sea oil platforms. The Tornado, in its ADV role, can operate from any 300-foot strip in the region, fly to a patrol station 300 to 400 miles away, remain there for more than two hours, carry out an interception, engage in a 10-minute air battle, and return to base with fuel to spare. Because the Tornado is equipped for aerial refueling, its duration in flight can be extended still further.

In operation, the Tornado, whether IDS or ADV, is a vital factor in preserving NATO air superiority over any potential European battlefield, and as such, it is also a vital factor in causing the Warsaw Pact to think twice about going to war.

GENERAL DYNAMICS
F-16 FALCON

A LIGHTWEIGHT FIGHTER WITH UNIVERSAL APPEAL

Like many of the great combat aircraft in service in the 1980s, the development of the F-16 began nearly a decade earlier. The roots of the F-16 program date to early 1972 and the US Air Force Lightweight Fighter (LWF) Prototype Program. The original idea was to develop a fast and highly maneuverable yet inexpensive fighter to supplement the F-15 in US Air Force service. All of the major US warplane builders (except McDonnell Douglas who already had the F-15 contract) submitted proposals for the LWF aircraft. The submissions of Boeing, Ling-Temco-Vought and Lockheed were all rejected as the Air Force, in August 1972, narrowed the competition down to two. It was decided to ask General Dynamics and Northrop to go forward with construction of two copies of each company's proposed aircraft. The General Dynamics Model Number 401 was given the USAF service test designation YF-16, while Northrop's P-600 was designated YF-17. To make its final selection of an LWF, the Air Force conducted a fly-off between the two aircraft.

The first General Dynamics YF-16 prototype was completed in December 1973 and first flown in February 1974, with the second YF-16 flying in May. The competi-

tion between the YF-16 and YF-17 consumed most of 1974. The competition was critically important to both firms because they each recognized that the winner would join McDonnell Douglas as one of the Air Force's key warplane suppliers for the next 15 to 20 years. Billions were at stake, along with two important reputations. General Dynamics had evolved from Convair, which had pioneered delta-winged supersonic aircraft in the US in the 1950s, and had built two of the Air Force's top second-generation interceptors, the F-102 Delta Dagger and F-106 Delta Dart. With these two planes, Convair had been the only manufacturer to have two operational aircraft among the celebrated Century series. Northrop, on the other hand, had no aircraft among the Century birds and had not built a first-line fighter for the Air Force since its first generation F-89 Scorpion. Northrop had, however, been responsible for the lightweight F-5 Tiger. Though fairly unsophisticated and designed explicitly for the export market, the F-5 was very close to what the Air Force said it wanted in the LWF.

In the end, the single-engined YF-16 defeated the twin-engined YF-17, and in January 1975 the USAF awarded the LWF laurel to General Dynamics with a con-

Below: An air-to-air right-underside view of two F-16 Fighting Falcons from the Black Widows squadron of Hill AFB, Utah, banking to the left.

Above: Next to the top-view silhouette of the F-16 are the military insignias of the user nations. *From left to right (top row):* Belgium, Denmark, Egypt, Greece, Israel, South Korea, The Netherlands, Norway. *Bottom row:* Pakistan, Turkey, Singapore, USA and Venezuela.

tract for 650 operational F-16s. In June 1975 further good news reached the Fort Worth, Texas headquarters of General Dynamics: four European countries, also shopping for a new-generation fighter, had decided on the F-16. It was announced that the air forces of Belgium, Denmark, Holland and Norway would purchase an aggregate of 348 of the new aircraft. General Dynamics had sold just short of one thousand aircraft in less than half a year.

General Dynamics began construction of the new aircraft in August 1975, with the first production aircraft ready for assembly in December. One year later, on 8 December 1976, the first production F-16A made its maiden flight. A month later the US Air Force placed an order for an additional 738 F-16s. May 1977 saw the first F-16A nonstop transcontinental flight, and August 1977 the first flight of the F-16B. The F-16B was identical to the F-16A except that it had a two-place cockpit. This aircraft, which was designed as a trainer, could also be used as a fighter.

While production was beginning in earnest, agreements were signed that gave the European nations ordering the F-16 a hand in its production as well. A five-nation memorandum of understanding had been signed in 1975 and the first co-production contract was signed in July 1976. Less than two years later, in February 1978, the first European assembly line was opened at the SONACA/SABCA facility in Gosselies near Charleroi in central Belgium. In April of the same year the

second European assembly line opened at the Fokker plant at Schiphol outside Amsterdam in the Netherlands. In July, the first major European-built components, wings from Belgium, were brought to the original Fort Worth, Texas assembly line for integration into a USAF F-16 being assembled there.

In the first decade of the F-16 Multinational Production Program, General Dynamics, the prime contractor, has distributed work among 5760 American subcontractors, while the 30 major European contractors have placed subcontracts with nearly 400 firms in Europe. In addition, nine subcontractors in Israel and two in Korea have had a share in the program.

January 1979 marked the beginning of the F-16's service career as the first aircraft were delivered to the US Air Force Tactical Air Command's 388th Tactical Fighter Wing at Hill AFB near Salt Lake City, Utah. In the same month, the Belgian air force (Force Aerienne Belge/Belgische Luchtmacht) took delivery of the first European-produced F-16. In June the Royal Netherlands air force (Konicklijk Luchtmacht Nederland) took delivery of its first F-16. Nine months later the Netherlands would announce that it would be purchasing 213 F-16s rather than the 102 originally planned.

In the meantime, Israel had, in August 1978, announced that it too would be joining the F-16 program with the purchase of 75 aircraft. The first of these were delivered in January 1980 from the Fort Worth assembly line, at the same time

Above: F-16s from the coproducing countries: The Netherlands *(foreground)*, USA, Belgium, Denmark and Norway (note powder burns on gun ports).

Opposite: An F-16 trailing vapor produced by a high-G climb in hot, humid air.

that Norway and Denmark were getting their first F-16s. The first four Israeli F-16s arrived in that country in July 1980 after an 11-hour, 6000-mile ferry from Pease AFB in New Hampshire. In June, Egypt, now at peace with Israel for the first time since the latter's creation in 1948, announced that its air force would become the seventh to acquire the F-16.

While the foreign marketing of the F-16 was proceeding at a good clip, production lines were filling squadrons with operational aircraft. The aircraft reached combat-ready status with the US Air Force in November 1980, and a year later there were 150 F-16s in that service. It is interesting to note that while many aircraft are assigned familiar names before they come off the drawing board as a marketing tool, the F-16 did not officially receive a name until July 1980. Officially adopted 18 months after first delivery, the F-16's name would be Fighting Falcon (or simply Falcon) after the mascot of the US Air Force Academy. In those 18 months the F-16 had managed to pick up a couple of unofficial names. When this author first 'met' the F-16 at Hill AFB in January 1979, pilots referred to it as the 'Viper,' though the most common unofficial name in later years would be 'Electric Jet.' The name Electric Jet is a reference to the fly-by-wire electronic controls that had completely replaced traditional hydraulic controls in the F-16.

By whatever name, by 1981 the F-16 had become an important feature in the air forces that were ordering it. In January 1981, only two months after the aircraft had achieved its initial operating capability (IOC) with the US Air Force, Belgium's 349th Squadron became the first NATO unit to become operational in Europe with the F-16. In March Falcons of the USAF Tactical Air Command's 388th Tactical Fighter Wing (TFW) were deployed to Norway in the first US Air Force overseas deployment of operational F-16s. As more and more Falcons became operational through 1981 their operational capabilities became more and more apparent. In June these remarkable new planes were entered in the Royal Air Force precision bombing competition at Lossiemouth, Scotland. In this competition the F-16, configured as a fighter-bomber, scored 7831 out of a possible 8000 points, or 97.9 percent. In August, a USAF Falcon destroyed a QF-102 target drone in the first guided launch of the new, all-weather, radar-guided Advanced Medium Range Air-to-Air Missile (AMRAAM). These exercises were, however, to be overshadowed in the summer of 1981 by the first utilization of the F-16 in live combat, when the Israelis used them in their fighter-bomber role to attack and destroy Iraq's Osirak nuclear reactor facility near Baghdad. This raid, discussed in detail in our section covering the Falcon in service, helped to fully demonstrate the combat effectiveness of the F-16.

In September 1981 the US Air Force Pacific Air Forces 8th Tactical Fighter Wing at Kunsan AB, South Korea became the first American overseas unit to become operational with Falcons. Two months later, South Korea became the eighth country to buy the F-16. Also in December 1981, Pakistan placed an order for the aircraft, becoming the second Arab nation to do so and the first since the Osirak raid. Egypt, the first in the Arab world to buy the aircraft, took delivery of the first of 40 in Fort Worth in January 1982, with the first 6 arriving in Egypt in March. In May the Egyptians would double their US-funded order to 80 aircraft.

Over the course of the next three years, the F-16 program went on to become the most successful international program of the 1980s involving a major combat aircraft. Pakistan received the first of her 40 aircraft in October 1982, less than a year after the initial order. Oil-rich Venezuela

became the first Western Hemisphere nation outside the United States to order a modern fourth-generation jet fighter in May 1982, as it signed a contract for 24 Falcons. The first of these would be delivered 18 months later. Turkey then ordered 160 in September 1983, while Greece, Turkey's traditional rival in the eastern Mediterranean, selected the aircraft in November 1984 after comparing it with several other major American and European aircraft. On the other side of the globe in Southeast Asia, Singapore and Thailand joined the nations ordering the F-16 in January and April 1985.

The F-16 continued to be an important aircraft to the original partners in the Multinational Production Program. In June 1982 the 200th European-built plane was delivered. The Fokker and SONACA/SABCA assembly lines had each produced exactly half of these aircraft. Throughout this period, Belgium, Denmark and the Netherlands each increased their original orders for F-16s,

with 370 having been produced in Europe by June 1985. In the United States the 1000th F-16 was produced in July 1983, and the 1000th *American-built* F-16 rolled off the line in June, 1985. This aircraft, an F-16C, marked the 831st production Falcon delivered to the US Air Force.

The US Air Forces in Europe became operational with the Falcon in July 1982 at Hahn AB in West Germany (50th TFW), and in April 1983 at Torrejon AB in Spain (401st TFW). Luke AFB in Arizona became a major F-16 training center in February 1983, and in July of the same year F-16s joined the Air National Guard at McEntire ANGB in South Carolina. The latter came as part of a new USAF program under which Air Guard units would receive the same first-line aircraft that were in service with Air Force units.

In March 1982, the US Air Force announced that their Thunderbirds flight demonstration team would begin the transition from T-38 trainers to F-16s, a transition which was completed by Nov-

GENERAL DYNAMICS F-16 FIGHTING FALCON

	F-16A*	F-16C**	F-16F***
Year first deployed:	1979	1984	1986–87 (scheduled delivery date)
Type:	Single-seat fighter	Single-seat fighter	Single-seat fighter
Power Plant:	One Pratt & Whitney F100-PW-200 afterburning turbofan @ 25,000 lb thrust	One Pratt & Whitney F100-PW-200 or General Electric F110-GE-100 afterburning turbofan @ 25,000 lb thrust each	One Pratt & Whitney F100 or General Electric F110 afterburning turbofan @ 25,000 lb thrust each
Wingspan:	32 ft 10 in	32 ft 10 in w/missiles; 31 ft w/o missiles	34 ft 4 in w/missiles; 32 ft 6 in w/o missiles
Length:	49 ft 4 in	49 ft 4 in	54 ft 3 in
Height:	16 ft 8 in	16 ft 8 in	17 ft 9 in
Gross Weight:	35,400 lb	37,500 lb	48,000 lb
Maximum Speed:	Mach 2 @ altitude; 1.2 @ sea level	Mach 2 @ altitude; Mach 1.2 @ sea level	Mach 2 @ altitude; Mach 1.2 @ sea level
Range:	340 mi normal; 2300 mi ferry w/external tanks	575 mi normal; 2300 mi ferry	575 mi normal; 2300 mi ferry
Service Ceiling:	60,000 ft	60,000 ft	60,000 ft
Fixed Armament:	One General Electric M61 20mm cannon	One General Electric M61 20mm cannon	One General Electric M61 20mm cannon
Users:	Belgium, Denmark, Egypt, Israel, South Korea, The Netherlands, Norway, Pakistan, USAF, Venezuela	Egypt, Greece, Israel, Singapore, South Korea, Turkey, USAF, USN	USAF (service test)
	*The F-16B is the two-seat trainer version of F-16A	**The F-16D is the two-seat trainer version of the F-16C	***The F-16F is a development of the F-16XL and F-16E test aircraft

Above: Hill AFB F-16s over the Wasatch Mountains.

Opposite above: An F-16 family portrait. The family includes *(from the top)* the AFTI/F-16, the F-16/79, the F-16C, the basic F-16A and the F-16XL, which went into production as the F-16F.

F-16C Falcon
(advanced version of F-16A)

F-16F Falcon
(based on F-16XL prototype)

F-16D Falcon
(two-seat version of F-16C)

ember 1982. The Thunderbirds opened their 1983 season with their new red, white and blue Falcons on 2 April of that year; by the time the season ended on 13 November, they had performed 78 shows at 65 sites before 16.5 million spectators. After the years of flying the unarmed T-38 trainers, these men, some of the best pilots in the US Air Force, were now flying a fully combat-capable aircraft. To quote Thunderbirds Commander Lt Col James Latham, the F-16 is:

'Impressive in its combat role and equally impressive in its demonstration role. In addition to aerobatic maneuvering proficiency, the aircrews maintain combat proficiency in air-to-surface tactics and in air-superiority maneuvers. The new Thunderbird organization actually uses some of the resources of a fully combat-ready F-16 squadron. Although the aircraft are painted in the traditional colors of the Thunderbirds, there are no modifications that in any way affect the combat capability of the aircraft. The F-16s used by the Thunderbirds can quickly be repainted and restored to combat configurations within hours. In crisis or wartime, the pilots and aircraft, along with maintenance and support personnel, would be rapidly reintegrated into their combat ready unit, the 430th Tactical Fighter Squadron, which is also stationed at Nellis AFB.'

THE FALCON IN DETAIL

Though originally conceived as an agile air-superiority fighter, the F-16's performance as a fighter-bomber has led to its now being considered a multimission aircraft, equally at home in air-to-air and air-to-surface operations. Compared with the aircraft it is replacing throughout the world, principally the F-104 and F-4, it has a much superior fuel efficiency, and roughly double the combat radius. The combination of these features has contributed to its success.

There are three basic types of operational F-16s. The first Falcon was the F-16A, which entered service in 1979 along with the F-16B, the two-seat trainer version of F-16A. Second, there are the F-16C and F-16D. The F-16C, which first flew on 19 June 1984 and joined the US Air Force in July, is nearly identical in outward appearance to the F-16A, but has vastly upgraded avionics and internal improvements. The F-16D has the same relationship to the F-16C that the F-16B has to the F-16A. The final type of F-16 is the F-16F, a radically different Falcon with a 'cranked arrow' delta wing, which first

Advanced avionics testing is being conducted with the AFTI/F-16, a modified F-16A. The view of the F-16A simulator at left shows the high-visibility cockpit, including the wide field-of-view HUD and two interactive multifunction head-down displays. The voice-commanded AFTI/F-16 goes far beyond the other F-16s in terms of avionics. The view of the AFTI/F-16 cockpit *(bottom left)* shows the control stick (positioned to the pilot's right) of the fly-by-wire system found in all F-16s. At *right*, an AFTI/F-16 is seen in flight.

flew in July 1982 under the designation F-16XL. It was briefly designated F-16E when submitted as a contender in the US Air Force Dual Role Fighter Demonstrator (DRFD) program, a contest it lost to the McDonnell Douglas F-15E in 1984.

The F-16 offers an assortment of technical and design innovations that previously had not been available in a single aircraft. These include fly-by-wire controls; a complete electronic flight control system with the control stick located on the side rather than the middle of the cockpit for easy and accurate control during high-G turns; a high-visibility cockpit and canopy; forebody strakes for controlled vortex lift; wing-fuselage blending to provide greater lift and fuel volume; and variable-wing camber with automatic, leading-edge maneuvering flaps. The aircraft components are 78.4 percent aluminum, 11 percent steel and 3.3 percent composites, with the balance made up of titanium and other materials.

With the advent of the F-16C, the Falcon offers a choice of either the Pratt & Whitney F100-PW-220, or General Electric F110-GE-100 turbofan engine. Beginning in 1986 the aircraft was equipped with a common engine bay to permit accommodation of either engine.

Other major innovations available in the F-16C that were not aboard the F-16A are the APG-68 multimode radar with increased range, expanded operating modes and sharper display resolution; a more advanced cockpit, with a wide-angle Head-Up Display (HUD) incorporating Forward-Looking Infrared (FLIR) video; avionics growth capacity in the form of expanded, higher speed computers, increased electrical power and open space for new hardware and wiring; and a 2100 lb increased payload weight capability. The F-16C also has the Low Altitude Navigation and Targeting for Night (LANTIRN) system, and the capacity to carry both the AMRAAM air-to-air and the AGM-65D IIR Maverick air-to-surface missiles.

The APG-68 radar is upgraded from the reliable APG-66 radar of the F-16A and B. It offers many improvements, such as a new programmable signal processor

(PSP), a new Dual-Mode Transmitter (DMT), and a new modular Low-Power Radio Frequency Unit (LPRF). These help to increase the range at which targets may be tracked. In an air-to-air mode, the APG-68 provides look-down capability against low-flying aircraft, very long-range target velocity search, four simultaneous scan patterns, the ability to establish tracking 'files' on 10 targets simultaneously, and the ability generally to track more targets with more accuracy. In its air-to-surface mode, the APG-68 provides a ground-terrain radar map with enhanced resolution, provides an ability to track moving targets on land or water even in high waves at sea, allows the pilot to freeze a 'frame' of the ground terrain radar map, all while providing air-to-ground ranging and computer guidance.

The basic armament of the F-16 includes a General Electric M61 20mm cannon located in the fuselage below the left side of the cockpit, and two AIM-9 Sidewinder air-to-air missiles on wingtip brackets. Beyond this, the F-16 can carry just about any type of ordnance in the modern western tactical repertoire. These include not only the Maverick and AMRAAM, but the AIM-7 Sparrow air-to-air missile, GBU-15 laser-guided 'smart' bombs, and a variety of conventional and nuclear weaponry.

The Falcon fleet is constantly being upgraded under what is called the F-16 Multinational Staged Improvement Program (MSIP), which has three stages designed to keep the Falcon on the leading edge of state-of-the-art aircraft technology. Stage I was aimed at wiring and structural improvements in the later

F-16A and B aircraft, and was concluded in March 1985. Stage II was that part of the F-16C and D program design that would permit these aircraft to be upgraded in the future. Stage III provides for retrofit of the advanced avionics systems into the F-16A through F-16D aircraft starting in 1987.

The F-16F program, which began as the F-16XL program in July 1982, consists of two delta-winged prototype demonstrator aircraft. A joint effort, the F-16XL aircraft modification was paid for by General Dynamics, while the US Air Force has contributed the cost of the flight testing. The program is aimed at helping to develop the technology that will be used in the next generation of American fighters. Designed in cooperation with the NASA Langley Research Center, the new wing has twice the area of the familiar F-16 wing, but produces lower drag and more lift. It also enables the aircraft to carry more fuel in its integral fuel tanks, and a more evenly distributed external weapons load.

One of the two F-16XL/F-16F prototypes is a single-seat version powered by the Pratt & Whitney F-100, while the other is a two-seater with a General Electric F110.

AFTI/F-16

Few advancements in avionics are more intriguing than those being tested in the Advanced Fighter Technology Integration (AFTI/F-16) program. First tested in 1982, the AFTI/F-16 (a modified F-16A testbed aircraft) began practical testing of control systems that had heretofore been dis-

cussed primarily in science fiction. At the heart of AFTI/F-16 are the digital flight-control systems and canards under the intake which permit the aircraft to turn without banking, to move side to side with the nose still pointed directly ahead, to ascend or descend without raising or lowering the nose, or to remain in level flight while raising or lowering the nose. While this is indeed innovative, it is particularly so when one considers that the pilot can control AFTI/F-16, and its weapons as well—without touching the controls—simply through voice commands.

Through the use of a prerecorded cassette, the AFTI/F-16 can be 'taught' to 'recognize' the pilot's voice and obey his commands. After initially solving the problem of how the pilot's tone of voice would affect the controls, Air Force engineers began working on screening background noise. The system permits the pilot to perform tasks such as changing radio frequencies and selecting weapons without having to look down for a switch in the cockpit. As the system is programmed to 'talk back,' it will become more important in providing fuel load updates and other warnings.

A helmet-mounted sight interfacing with an infrared target tracker and laser target ranger permit the pilot to attack a target just by looking at it. Once the target is lined up with the helmet-mounted sight, the flight-control computer automatically steers the aircraft in pursuit. When the computer determines that the target is within range, it can be programmed to automatically fire. The technology available in the AFTI/F-16 program opens broad new horizons in warplane design, and the pilots of the AFTI/F-16 program will help the designers determine how best to mold this technology to real-world, real-time combat situations.

THE FALCON IN SERVICE

The F-16's first taste of combat came on 7 June 1981 as eight recently delivered Falcons took off from Israel's secret Etzion AB on the occupied Sinai peninsula and headed across the Gulf of Aqaba toward Saudi Arabia. The target for the day, located far across the burning sands of northern Saudi Arabia and deep within the Republic of Iraq, was the French-built, 70-megawatt Osirak nuclear power plant at Tammuz near the Iraqi capital of Baghdad. The raid had been ordered because Israeli intelligence had reason to believe that Iraq would be able, within months, to build nuclear weapons at the facility. They reasoned that by as early as July, highly radioactive fuel would be in place, and a raid would unleash a cloud of death over nearby Baghdad. To do nothing, said Israeli Prime Minister Menachem Begin, would put Israel in the shadow of a nuclear 'holocaust.'

The raid had been under secret consideration since October 1980, with a mission featuring Israeli F-4 Phantoms planned for as early as November. Ironically, Iran, which was then engaged in a full-scale war with Iraq, had actually carried out an unsuccessful attack on the reactor in September 1980 using F-4s. Throughout the winter and spring of 1981 the Israeli air force was going ahead with contingency planning. Under cover of the chaos created by the Iran-Iraq war, reconnaissance flights were carried out over the site, and a full-scale model was constructed in the Sinai against which dozens of bomb runs were flown.

Having replaced the F-4s for the mission, the eight F-16s took off at 4:40 pm and crossed into Arab air space. They were detected by Jordanian radar, but the pilots convinced the Jordanian controllers, in perfect Arabic, that they were Arab aircraft. One-half hour after takeoff, they crossed into Iraq and headed down the Euphrates River Valley toward the target. Twenty minutes later, the eight Falcons dropped out of the setting sun and began, one by one, to slam their one-ton bombs into the concrete dome of the reactor. Antiaircraft artillery coughed to life, but it was too late—the Israelis were gone, with nary a loss.

The reactor was a total loss, with tons of

Above: One of the Israeli F-16s that took part in the 1981 Osirak raid flies over the famed Masada.

Right: This 1989 photo by Gary Tolbert shows an F-16 test bed in green-camouflage paint scheme in a close air support configuration. The Falcon Eye FLIR sensor ball, visible just forward of the canopy, relays an infrared image to the pilot's helmet-mounted display.

F-16 Program Status

	Delivered Through September 1989	Total Contracted Through September 1989	First Operational Acquisition
US Air Force	1545*	1859	1979
US Navy	26	26	1987
Belgium	136	160	1979
Denmark	58	70	1980
Netherlands	184	213	1979
Norway	72	74	1980
Israel	150	210	1981
Egypt	80	122	1981
Pakistan	40	51	1982
Venezuela	24	24	1983
Korea	36	40	1986
Turkey	34	160	1987
Greece	28	40	1988
Thailand	12	18	1988
Singapore	8	8	1988
Indonesia	1	12	1989
Bahrain	0	12	1990
Totals	**2434**	**3099**	

*US Air Force totals exclude eight prototype and development aircraft and two F-16XLs currently operated by NASA as test and evaluation aircraft. As of September 1989, 1545 out of 1859 that were funded had been delivered, and the Air Force had requested Congressional approval for the purchase of an additional 750 through fiscal year 1994.

concrete and at least one unexploded bomb (which may have been intentional to prevent tampering with the wreck) piled on the reactor core. For Iraq, the raid meant an end to its ambition to become a nuclear power. For Israel, it meant a storm of worldwide controversy, but for the Falcon, it meant an unqualified tactical success in its baptism by fire.

Like the Israeli air force, the US Air Force also designated most of its Falcons as fighter-bombers, but in 1986 the Air Force found itself with a need for a lightweight air defense fighter to augment its heavier and more expensive F-15s, as well as its F-107 fleet, the latter of which was in its third decade of service.

The choices were the Northrop F-20 Tigershark, a follow-on to the F-5 Tiger, and a variant of the F-16. The former was not in service with any air service anywhere in the world and, although it had received rave reviews from test pilots (including Chuck Yeager), it existed only in the form of a company-owned demonstrator.

In November 1986, the Air Force announced that it would take 270 F-16As, as they were replaced by F-16Cs, and retrofit them as air defense fighters. This retrofit would be the major part of an upgrade of 425 F-16As and F-16Bs that would take place at the Ogden Air Logistics Center at Hill AFB, Utah. The F-16A

interceptors would roll out of the Ogden Center with provision for Westinghouse AN/APG-66 radar and able to participate in the Rockwell Navstar Global Positioning System (GPS). Offensive hardware would include the AIM-7 Sparrow and AIM-120 AMRAAM air-to-air missiles, as well as the AIM-9s currently used on F-16s.

In 1988, two years after the Air Force's selection of the F-16 as an interceptor, General Dynamics proposed the Falcon as a solution to the Air Force requirement for a Close Air Support/Battlefield Air Interdiction (CAS/BAI) aircraft to replace the Fairchild Republic A-10 Warthog that was being phased out of service. Such aircraft would be designated A-16 and would incorporate avionics and armament demonstrated on test flights in 1988 and 1989. The former included the Falcon Eye Forward Looking Infrared Radar (FLIR), which actually could be *steered* by Cat's Eyes night vision goggles built into the pilot's helmet. The million dollars per

unit Falcon Eye FLIR system included terrain following radar, laser designator/rangefinder and boresight correlator for automatic hand-off of targets to AGM-65 Maverick air-to-ground missiles. Other armament would include bombs, rockets and 30mm gun pods.

By 1989 the US Air Force had 1015 F-16s in active service, 214 assigned to the Air National Guard and 58 in the US Air Force Reserve. Air Force units included Tactical Fighter Squadrons of the Tactical Air Command, the Pacific Air Forces and the US Air Forces in Europe, as well as the Air Force Thunderbirds aerobatic demonstration team.

The Falcon is the most successful major export fighter in years. In addition to those in service with the US Air Force, over 400 are also in service in Belgium, Denmark, the Netherlands and Norway, which were the original participating countries, as well as many others (*see chart*). In October 1987, Japanese Defense Minister Yuko Kurihara and US Secre-

tary of Defense Caspar Weinberger reached an agreement under which the Japanese Air Self Defense Force (JASDF) would use the F-16 as the basis for the development of the FS-X strike fighter. The FS-X would be developed primarily by Mitsubishi, with General Dynamics having roughtly a 40 percent share.

The US Navy has also selected the small and maneuverable Falcon under the F-16N designation for aggressor training in its Top Gun exercises. Being dissimilar in appearance to familiar Navy aircraft, the F-16N would be used to simulate Soviet bloc tactics in mock air battles with regular Navy units. The decision of the Navy to buy a plane named after the Air Force Academy mascot marked the first time that the Navy had purchased a major first-line jet that was already in service with the US Air Force. It was also the first time since the Air Force went for the Navy's F-4 Phantom that the two services would be using the same type of major high performance fighter.

SAAB
VIGGEN

THE VERSATILE SWEDE

During World War II, Sweden's carefully nurtured neutrality helped spare her the horrors of that terrible conflict. In the aftermath of that war, this Scandinavian kingdom resolved that, to safeguard her precious neutrality, she must develop a fully independent arms industry. This was to include even the most complex of systems, including high-performance jet aircraft. The task of developing these new aircraft went to the Svenska Aeroplan Aktiebolaget (Swedish Airplane Company) or Saab, a firm which had only just delivered its first planes in 1940.

The first Saab postwar aircraft (excluding the 1947 conversion of its wartime model 21 to jet power) was the Saab 29 Tunnan (Barrel). This cumbersome but efficient first-generation fighter was followed by the Saab 32 Lansen (Lance), which was in turn followed by the highly sophisticated, delta-winged third-generation Saab 35 Draken (Dragon). Though intended first and foremost for Sweden's defense, these aircraft types also enjoyed limited export sales to other neutral countries such as Austria, and to other Scandinavian countries such as Denmark and Finland.

As had been the case in the earlier generations, Sweden began work on its fourth-generation combat aircraft before most other countries with much larger aircraft industries. Like the Saab 35 before it, the new aircraft would have to be equally adept as a Mach 2 interceptor or as a Mach 1 fighter-bomber, and would have to be capable of operating from short, unimproved runways in Sweden's most rugged areas. Work began on the concept for the new aircraft as early as 1961, with the resulting Saab 37 Viggen (Thunderbolt) making its first flight in February 1967.

The first production Viggen, the AJ37 fighter-bomber version, rolled out in October 1970, joining the *Flygvapnet* (Swedish Air Force) in 1971. With the Draken still in place as its leading interceptor, the *Flygvapnet* moved first to develop other versions of Viggen. As the AJ37 moved in to replace the much older 32 fighter-bombers, three ancillary model 37 subtypes were brought on line. These were the SK37 two-seat combat-capable trainer, the SF37 photo reconnaissance variant (with its distinctive nose-mounted

Above right: Next to the top-view silhouette of the Swedish-built Viggen is the military insignia of the only user nation, Sweden.

Below: A *Flygvapnet* Viggen AJ37 in camouflage paint scheme. The Viggen fighter was built for very high speed at low altitude.

Bottom left: The Viggen carries Sidewinder and Sky Flash missiles as well as air-to-surface rockets and an automatic 30mm cannon.

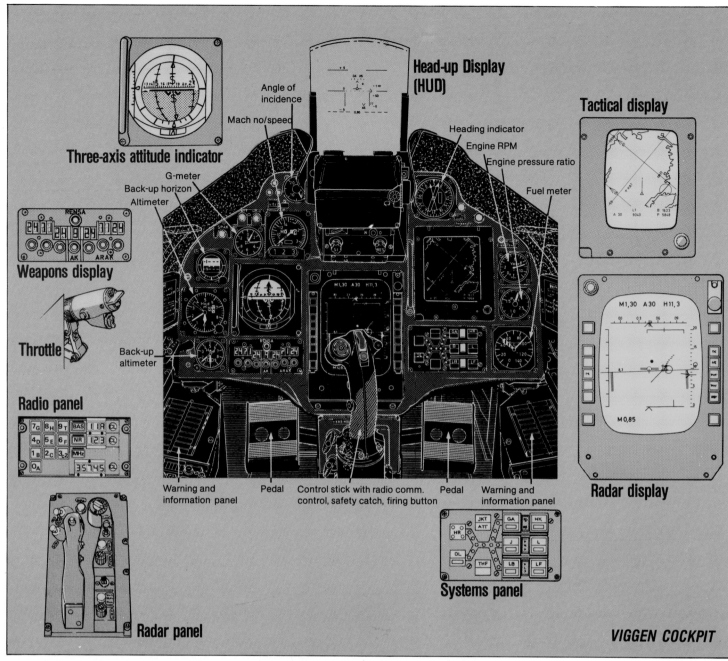

Three-axis attitude indicator

Angle of incidence

Mach no/speed

Head-up Display (HUD)

Heading indicator
Engine RPM
Engine pressure ratio
Fuel meter

Tactical display

G-meter
Back-up horizon
Altimeter

Weapons display

Throttle

Back-up altimeter

Radio panel

Radar display

Warning and information panel

Pedal

Control stick with radio comm. control, safety catch, firing button

Pedal

Warning and information panel

Systems panel

Radar panel

VIGGEN COCKPIT

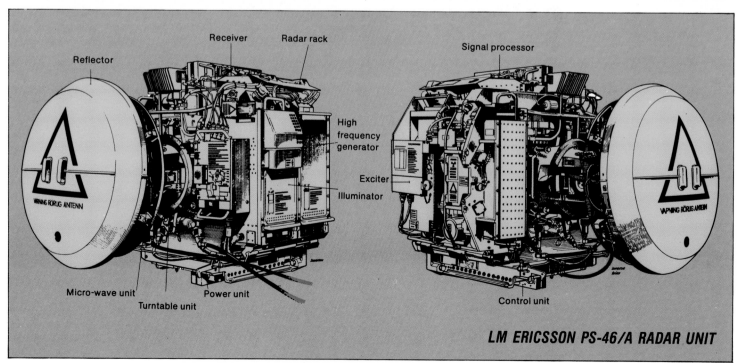

Reflector

Receiver

Radar rack

Signal processor

High frequency generator

Exciter

Illuminator

Micro-wave unit

Turntable unit

Power unit

Control unit

LM ERICSSON PS-46/A RADAR UNIT

During a recent joint Soviet/Swedish air forces exchange visit, Soviet Col G Zadvinsi inspected a Viggen *(right)*, and *(above)* Swedish pilot Major Christer Hjort made a low-level pass over the heads of some Soviet officers.

camera system) and the SH37, a maritime reconnaissance variant almost identical to the SF37 except for certain specialized avionics systems designed for over-water use.

The go-ahead for the JA37 JaktViggen (Fighting Thunderbolt) interceptor variant was given in 1972, but development funds were not appropriated until 1974 after the first flight of an AJ37 modified to JA37 standard on 4 June of that year. The first all-new JA37 flew on 15 December 1975, but full-scale production did not begin until October 1977 and the first aircraft did not become operational until 1980, much behind schedule. While production of the early Saab 37 variants concluded in 1980, the company, now Saab-Scania, is expected to keep the JA37 assembly line open until the end of the 1980s.

THE VIGGEN IN DETAIL

Except for a handful of two-seat SK37 trainers, the Viggen series is entirely composed of structurally similar single-seat, single-engine warplanes. The most unique of the Viggen's design features are its high-angle delta wings and canard foreplanes. The aircraft was one of the first jet aircraft to be designed with forward-mounted canard elevators instead of conventionally mounted elevators and as such was considered quite a revolutionary design. It is this arrangement that helps give the Viggen its all-important short-takeoff capability. Another factor is the powerful Swedish-built Volvo Flygmotor RM8 turbofan engine. The RM8 is based on the American Pratt & Whitney JT8D turbofan used on much larger commercial aircraft, but is equipped with a Swedish-developed afterburner which helps give the Viggen more-than-adequate power for short takeoffs, Mach 1 speed at low altitude and Mach 2 speed at intercept altitudes. All the Viggen subtypes are fitted with the RM8A except the JA37 which uses the slightly larger and more powerful RM8B. Short field landings are accomplished through the use of a large tail-mounted thrust-reverser system which permits the Viggen to practically drop out of the sky in a 1300-foot roll-out, less than half the distance required for its own con-

SAAB VIGGEN

	JA37 Viggen	AJ37 Viggen
Year first deployed:	1980	1971
Type:	Single-seat interceptor	Single-seat attack aircraft
Power Plant:	One Volvo Flygmotor RM8B afterburning turbofan @ 28,150 lb thrust	One Volvo Flygmotor RM8A afterburning turbofan @ 26,015 lb thrust
Wingspan:	34 ft 9 in	34 ft 9 ft
Length:	53 ft 11 in	53 ft 5 in
Height:	18 ft 4 in	18 ft 4 in
Wing Area:	495 sq ft	495 sq ft
Gross Weight:	37,480 lb	35,275 lb
Empty Weight:	26,015 lb	26,015 lb
Maximum Speed:	Mach 2 @ altitude Mach 1.1 @ sea level	Mach 2 @ altitude Mach 1.1 @ sea level
Range:	620 mi tactical radius	620 mi tactical radius
Service Ceiling:	60,000 ft	60,000 ft
Fixed Armament:	One Oerliken KCA 30mm cannon	None
Users:	Sweden	Sweden

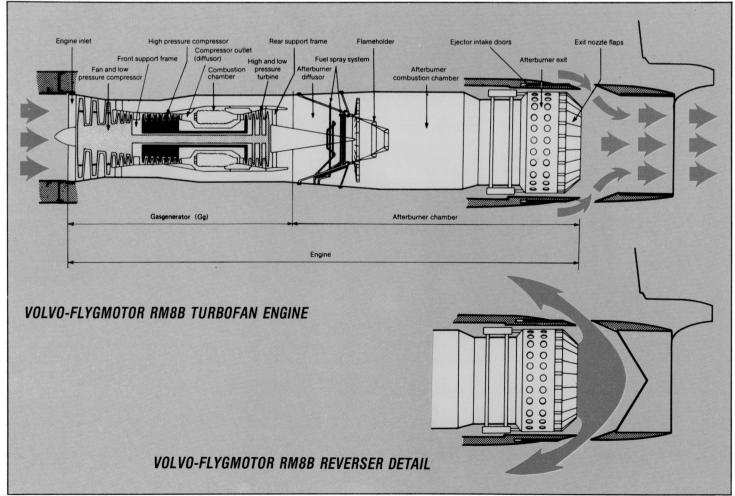

VOLVO-FLYGMOTOR RM8B TURBOFAN ENGINE

VOLVO-FLYGMOTOR RM8B REVERSER DETAIL

ventional landing. *Flygvapnet* pilots also train for aircraft carrier-type landings using the thrust reversers the way a carrier pilot would use the arresting cable. This type of training is important because Sweden is small enough that, in time of war, all of its air bases could be put out of action quickly by an aggressor and *Flygvapnet* aircraft would need to use short, straight stretches of highway as well as open fields for landing and operating bases.

The centerpiece of the Viggen's avionics system is the LM Ericsson pulse-doppler radar. The AJ37 carries the Ericsson UAP 1011 system optimized for ground attack, while the UAP 1023 of the JA37 is designed with look-down shoot-down capability for air attack missions. The cockpit contains a Head-Up Display (HUD) system and the unique Honeywell/Saab-Scania SA07 Digital Flight-Control System for ease of operation in a combat situation. Like the American F-15 Eagle and many other fourth-generation warplanes, the Viggen was designed around the pilot, designed to respond immediately and smoothly to the pilot's commands.

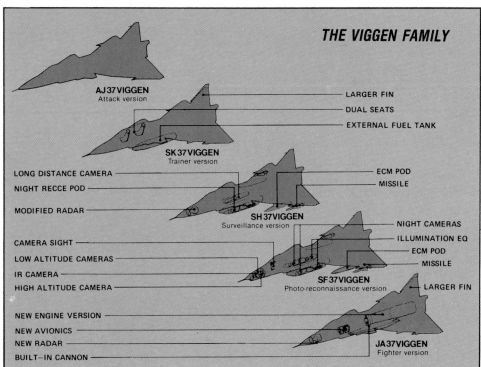

THE VIGGEN FAMILY

AJ 37 VIGGEN
Attack version

SK 37 VIGGEN
Trainer version

LARGER FIN
DUAL SEATS
EXTERNAL FUEL TANK

LONG DISTANCE CAMERA
NIGHT RECCE POD
MODIFIED RADAR

SH 37 VIGGEN
Surveillance version

ECM POD
MISSILE

CAMERA SIGHT
LOW ALTITUDE CAMERAS
IR CAMERA
HIGH ALTITUDE CAMERA

SF 37 VIGGEN
Photo-reconnaissance version

NIGHT CAMERAS
ILLUMINATION EQ
ECM POD
MISSILE

NEW ENGINE VERSION
NEW AVIONICS
NEW RADAR
BUILT-IN CANNON

JA 37 VIGGEN
Fighter version

LARGER FIN

The Viggen carries no built-in armament, but has the capacity for a wide variety of weaponry, which can be mounted on seven attachment points. Among these are the Oerlikon KCA 30mm single-barreled cannon which can be carried in a detachable gun pack mounted on the center

fuselage. The gun pack is attached as standard equipment to the JA37 and as such it is often considered to be fixed armament on this aircraft. Other types of armament include a wide range of air-to-ground weapons available for the AJ37 and of air-to-air weapons for the JA37. The seven attachment points beneath the aircraft can also accommodate fuel tanks, electronic countermeasures pods and reconnaissance pods.

The air-to-air repertoire includes the British Aerospace Sky Flash and the American AIM-9 Sidewinder (Swedish designation Rb24). The air-to-ground repertoire, which is available to the SK37 as well AJ37 includes such guided weapons as the American AGM065 Maverick (Swedish designation Rb75) as well the Swedish Rb04 anti-ship and Rb05 air-to-ground missiles. These attack-configured Viggens can also carry unguided rockets and conventional bombs.

THE VIGGEN IN SERVICE

While foreign military sales are not nearly as important to Sweden as they are to other Western European nations such as France, Saab-Scania has made several attempts to sell the Viggen abroad. The first and most important instance wherein the aircraft was a contender was in the mid-1970s when Belgium, Denmark, Holland and Norway were looking for a replacement for their aging fleet of F-104s. Despite Sweden's stringent arms-export regulations, one would think that there would have been a chance to sell the Viggen to a group of nations, half of whom were Scandinavian like Sweden. In the end, however, the General Dynamics F-16 became the new front-line fighter on NATO's northern tier. Shortly thereafter, the Viggen was being considered, along with the French Mirage F1 and Anglo-French SEPECAT Jaguar, to answer India's requirement for a long-range fighter bomber. In the end, this contest was lost because the United States refused (for security reasons) to permit export of the modified American JT8D engine, despite the fact that the basic JT8D was used on commercial jetliners. Another potential customer, Austria, looked at the Viggen, but decided to forego arming itself with any sort of sophisticated later-generation aircraft because of cost.

Having made no foreign sales during the first half of the 1980s, Saab-Scania relied on the *Flygvapnet* as its sole customer for the Viggen. At the decade's mid-point Sweden's air arm had five combat squadrons, six reconnaissance squadrons with a mix of 52 SF37 and SH37 aircraft and a single training squadron with 15 SK37s. Four interceptor squadrons were operational with 70 JA37s, and an additional 76 JA37 JaktViggens were on order for delivery through the balance of the decade.

This light-grey JaktViggen interceptor blends into the clouds. The US F-15 and RAF Tornado interceptors have similar color schemes.

McDONNELL DOUGLAS
F/A-18 HORNET

THE LIGHTWEIGHT FIGHTER-BOMBER

The origin of the F/A-18 Hornet can be traced to precisely the same point as that of the F-16. This common starting point was the US Air Force Lightweight Fighter (LWF) program of the early 1970s. Within the context of that program a number of America's leading builders of combat aircraft submitted proposals for a relatively inexpensive lightweight fighter to complement the large and expensive McDonnell Douglas F-15, which was intended to serve as a first-line USAF air-superiority fighter. Two of these firms, General Dynamics and Northrop, came out on top in the first round of evaluations, and in April 1972 were each asked to build a pair of actual prototype aircraft based on their proposals. The General Dynamics aircraft received the US Air Force service test designation YF-16, while the Northrop entry was designated YF-17. The two types were thoroughly tested throughout 1974, with General Dynamics emerging the winner on 13 January 1975 with the award of a contract calling for series production of the F-16.

Northrop was left with a pair of YF-17s into which they had poured a great deal of research and development resources. At the same time, the US Navy was facing a problem similar to that of the Air Force. As the Air Force had its potent but expensive F-15 and needed a smaller, less ex-pensive complement, the Navy had its potent, expensive F-14 coming on line. Yet the F-14 was designed as a carrier-based air-superiority fighter just as the F-15 had been designed as a land-based air-superiority fighter. The Navy needed a plane to do what the F-16 was expected to do for the Air Force. They needed a lightweight, inexpensive fighter that could double as an attack plane.

To meet its VFAX (Fighter/Attack, Experimental) requirement the Navy looked at a number of options, including the F-16, a cheaper F-14 and an improved version of the older third-generation McDonnell Douglas F-4 Phantom. Northrop saw in the VFAX a second chance for the F-17 project, but having had no experience with the specialized art of carrier-plane design, the firm had to turn to a collaborator. This collaborator would be McDonnell Douglas. The McDonnell component of McDonnell Douglas had built the Navy's first carrier-based jet fighter back in the 1940s and had gone on to build a series of such aircraft culminating in the F-4, which had been the top all-around carrier-based combat jet in history.

The result of the Northrop-McDonnell Douglas collaboration won the VFAX contract and became the Navy's next fighter under the designation F-18 *and* it

Above: The third F/A-18 prototype lands on the USS America during the first carrier tests.

Below: The Australian Hornet and the Canadian CF-18 (bottom) on display.

became the Navy's newest attack aircraft under the designation A-18, although for convenience it is referred to as the F/A-18 because the two types are virtually identical. In service, however, the Navy will use its F/A-18s primarily as attack aircraft, while the US Marine Corps will use the aircraft mainly in the fighter role.

Nicknamed Hornet, the F/A-18 is very similar to the YF-17 in overall layout and appearance, but it has more powerful engines and redesigned, heavy-duty landing gear. Under the details of their collaboration McDonnell Douglas would be the prime contractor, with Northrop serving as the 'major airframe subcontractor,' receiving roughly 40 percent of the airframe portion of the project. The engine contract went to General Electric, who had built the engines used in the YF-17 prototypes.

The Hornet made its first flight on 18 November 1978 with McDonnell Douglas test pilot Jack Krings at the controls. Despite early teething troubles and a round of late-1970s inflation that increased project cost, the test program proceeded reasonably well. The first test flights to and from an aircraft carrier took place aboard the USS America during October and November 1979 and were termed 'the most successful sea trials in naval aviation history.' Weapons trials began in December 1979, and over the course of the next year the Hornet was successfully tested with both air-to-air and air-to-ground munitions.

After the experimental phase of its development, the Hornet entered squadron service on 13 November 1980 with the US Navy's VFA-125 (aka the *Rough*

Raiders) at Lemoore NAS in California's central valley. The job of VFA-125 would be to train Hornet pilots in preparation for the introduction of the aircraft into carrier-based squadrons. The first US Marine Corps squadron to receive the F/A-18 was the *Black Knights* of VMFA 314 at El Toro MCAS in Southern California. The first Hornets to be permanently assigned to aircraft carrier duty joined carrier squadrons VFA-25 and VFA-113 aboard the USS *Constellation* in 1983.

While McDonnell Douglas was busily developing the F/A-18 for the US Navy and Marine Corps, the company was also looking for an export market for the plane. The first foreign government to select the Hornet was Canada, who hadn't procured a first-line fighter aircraft since it acquired its second-generation F-101s and F-104s over a decade before. The Canadian Armed Forces selected the F/A-18 over the F-16 because they felt the latter's single engine was a limiting factor and because the F/A-18 was developed for service over vast reaches of open sea, an environment that more closely approximates the sparsely populated terrain of Canada than does the European environment for which the F-16 was developed. Designated CF-18, the Hornet first entered squadron service in Canada in 1983 with the 410 Squadron at Canadian Forces Base Bagotville in Quebec.

The second Hornet export customer was the Royal Australian Air Force which has the same vast open domestic terrain as Canada and the same over-water operational requirements as those of the US Navy. Under the terms of the contract, Australia would buy 75 F/A-18s with the first two being built entirely by McDonnell Douglas in St Louis, Missouri and the remainder being assembled by the Australian Government Aircraft Factory at Avalon. The first two RAAF Hornets, two-seat versions, were completed in October 1984 and delivered to the US Navy's Lemoore NAS where Australian pilots would first be trained to fly the new aircraft. On 17 May 1985, initial pilot training completed, these two Hornets arrived at RAAF Williamstown flying the 7700 miles from Lemoore without stopping. Having been refueled several times enroute by US Air Force KC-10 tankers, the two F/A-18s had completed the longest Hornet flight to date. These two aircraft, flown by RAAF Wing Commander

Right: An early all-grey US Navy Hornet with low-visibility insignia. The Navy got what it wanted in the McDonnell Douglas F/A-18 Hornet—a reliable and easily maintained warplane.

McDONNELL DOUGLAS
F/A-18 HORNET

Year first deployed:	1982
Type:	Single-seat carrier-based combat/strike aircraft
Power Plant:	Two General Electric F404-GE-400 afterburning turbofans @ 16,000 lb thrust each
Wingspan:	40 ft 8 in
Length:	56 ft
Height:	15 ft 4 in
Wing Area:	400 sq ft
Gross Weight:	33,580 lb
Maximum Speed:	Mach 1.8 @ altitude
Range:	2300 mi ferry
Service Ceiling:	50,000 ft
Fixed Armament:	One General Electric M61 20mm cannon
Users:	Australia, Canada, Spain, USMC, USN

Brian Robinson and Flight Lieutenant Gus Larard in one aircraft and Squadron Leader Laurie Evans and Flight Lieutenant Gerry O'Brien in the other, completed the record-breaking flight in 15 hours.

Once at Williamstown, the two aircraft joined the third Australian F/A-18. The latter was the first domestically assembled F/A-18 which had first flown on 26 February 1985 and which had joined the RAAF at Williamstown on 4 May.

Having signed a contract with McDonnell Douglas on 31 May 1983, the Spanish government by-passed the F-16 and became the fourth customer, and the first in Europe, to buy the F/A-18. As a replacement for the F-4 Phantoms of Spain's *Ejercito del Aire,* the first Hornets entered service in 1986.

THE HORNET IN DETAIL

Originally designed as an inexpensive lightweight fighter, the Hornet evolved into a moderately expensive middleweight fighter-bomber. It is constructed mostly of aluminum, (50 percent by weight) but with its tail surfaces and a large part of its wing surfaces composed of graphite/epoxy composite materials. McDonnell Douglas, the prime contractor, manufactures the forward fuselage, wings and horizontal tail surfaces, while Northrop, who originated the project, builds the twin vertical tail surfaces and the portions of fuselage aft of and including the wing roots.

The aircraft is powered by a pair of General Electric F404 turbofan engines which are in the same thrust class as the much larger and heavier J79 turbojet engine used in the F-4 Phantom. The F404, which was developed especially for the Hornet, has gone on to be specified for use in the Northrop F-20 Tigershark and the Saab-Scania Gripen, Sweden's projected lightweight air-superiority fighter.

The Hornet (except for a handful of two-seat trainers) has a single-place cockpit designed with extensive use of digital electronic displays and, like the other aircraft of its generation, a Head-Up Display (HUD). Below the HUD, three CRT screens can be programmed to display a wide variety of data. The avionics include the Hughes APG-65 multimode radar and a Forward-Looking Infrared (FLIR) system for nighttime operations.

The armament of the Hornet varies as to whether its role is as an F-18 or an A-18, but either scenario includes the M61 six-barreled 20mm rotary cannon located in the top of the forward fuselage just ahead of the cockpit. While the cannon constitutes the plane's only fixed armament, there are seven attachment points under the fuselage and wings for a variety of external stores and one on each wingtip for AIM-9 Sidewinder air-to-air missiles. The weapons that can be carried include many types of conventional bombs and unguided rockets, as well as the AGM-62 and AGM-65 Maverick air-to-surface missiles, the AGM-88 HARM anti-radar missile and the AIM-7 Sparrow air-to-air missile. Another important munition is the AGM-109 Harpoon, a missile specifically designed for use against enemy surface ships.

THE HORNET IN SERVICE

The US Navy and Marine Corps, both components of the US Department of the Navy, are the primary customers for the McDonnell Douglas/Northrop F/A-18 Hornet. Originally the Navy Department

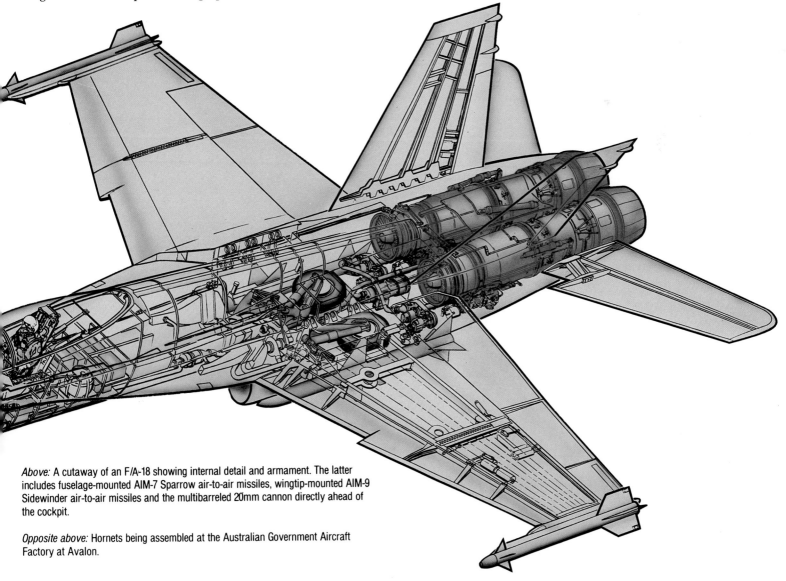

Above: A cutaway of an F/A-18 showing internal detail and armament. The latter includes fuselage-mounted AIM-7 Sparrow air-to-air missiles, wingtip-mounted AIM-9 Sidewinder air-to-air missiles and the multibarreled 20mm cannon directly ahead of the cockpit.

Opposite above: Hornets being assembled at the Australian Government Aircraft Factory at Avalon.

had stated its requirement for 1845 of these aircraft, but this number was revised downward to 1366 because of budgetary limitations. At the beginning of 1985, the US Navy had 2 of its 38 attack squadrons equipped with 25 Hornets and an additional 60 aircraft in transition units. The Marine Corps had 4 fighter squadrons with 48 Hornets and plans to replace the F-4s in its 8 remaining fighter squadrons. The Marines also had 20 Hornets in training units and 80 on order.

The Canadian Armed Forces' plan was to have 54 of 138 CF-18s in service with three squadrons by mid-1987. Two of these squadrons would be assigned to the North American Air Defense Command (NORAD) and would be based at CFB Bagotville (which had been flying Hornets since 1983) and CFB Cold Lake in northeastern Alberta. The third squadron is 409 Squadron at Baden-Sollingen in West Germany. Part of Canada's commitment to NATO, 409 Squadron was equipped

with Lockheed CF-104 Starfighters prior to conversion to Hornets.

By mid-1985, the Royal Australian Air Force had received the first three of its planned complement of 75 Hornets. Spain, NATO's newest member and the first European Hornet customer, had planned to order 144 F-18s, but this number was reduced to a firm commitment for 72 with an option on 12 more. The first delivery of the Spanish Hornets, designated EF-18, was scheduled to take place during 1986.

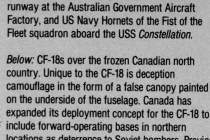

Left: An EF-18 Hornet with Spanish markings.

Left from bottom: A completed Hornet on the runway at the Australian Government Aircraft Factory, and US Navy Hornets of the Fist of the Fleet squadron aboard the USS *Constellation.*

Below: CF-18s over the frozen Canadian north country. Unique to the CF-18 is deception camouflage in the form of a false canopy painted on the underside of the fuselage. Canada has expanded its deployment concept for the CF-18 to include forward-operating bases in northern locations as deterrence to Soviet bombers. Previous plans had CF-18s operating solely from main bases, such as Cold Lake and Bagotville.

DASSAULT-BREGUET
MIRAGE 2000

STATE-OF-THE-ART DELTA

The small, clean delta-winged fighter that first flew at Istres, France on 10 March 1978 was a carefully planned warplane from a well-established lineage of such aircraft. Founded by Marcel Bloch (aka Marcel Dassault) shortly after World War II, Avions Dassault quickly became France's leading builder of jet warplanes. The Dassault design philosophy called for each aircraft type to be part of an evolutionary pattern rather than a radical departure from its predecessor. The result was a series of well-defined 'families' of aircraft. During the 1950s and early 1960s Dassault's Mystere and Etendard families formed the centerpiece of the French *Armee de l'Air* and an important element in French arms sales abroad.

As early as the mid-1950s the third and most important Dassault 'family' was emerging from the drawing board. The first of the Mirage family, Mirage I, appeared in 1955, followed by the similar but more refined Mirage III a year later, with Mirage II having not been produced. The early Mirages were tactical fighter/fighter-bomber aircraft distinguished by a pure delta wing of the type being used by Convair in the United States for their F-102 and F-106. The Mirage III was the standard production version and proved very successful for Dassault (which was soon to merge with Breguet). Over 1500 aircraft were sold to 25 countries. The tactical Mirages were followed by the half-again-larger Mirage IV, a delta-winged strategic bomber sold only to the French *Armee de l'Air*. The Mirage V (5) was a variation on the Mirage III. The next Mirage, the F1, bore many physical simi-

Below: Mirage 2000Cs of the *Armee de l'Air* taxi as they prepare for a twilight takeoff.

Bottom: The second prototype of the Mirage 2000, in company markings, test fires a Matra 530 missile.

Above: Next to the top-view silhouette of the Mirage 2000 are the military insignias of the user nations. From left to right: Egypt, France, Peru and Abu Dhabi.

Above: A Mirage 2000, in camouflage blues, with orange Matra 530 and Magic 2 air-to-air missiles.

Below: The first prototype of the two-seat nuclear strike version, Mirage 2000N, in flight.

larities to the Mirage III except that it had a shoulder-mounted conventional rather than delta wing. Though generally regarded as a successful aircraft, having sold in 10 countries, it failed to capture the important Belgium/Holland/Denmark/Norway sale that went to the General Dynamics F-16.

It was against this backdrop that Dassault-Breguet began working on a successor to the earlier Mirages, notably the Mirage III. The first such concept came in response to the *Armee de l'Air* Future Combat Aircraft *(Avion de Combat Futur)* program. The Dassault-Breguet ACF project was abruptly canceled in

1975 when the government decided it wanted a lighter single-engined fighter rather than a large twin-engined aircraft. The company's engineers scrambled back to the drawing board and created a new concept which was accepted by the *Armee de l'Air* on 18 December 1975. Designated Mirage 2000, the design of the new aircraft went back to the delta wing common to the early Mirages but not used on either the F1 or ACF. It would be roughly the same size as the Mirage III, but would contain vastly improved internal systems. Like the Mirage III, the new aircraft was a single-seat, single-engine fighter capable of performing interception, reconnaissance, ground support and long-range strike missions.

Having been built at the St Cloud facility of Dassault-Breguet, the first Mirage 2000 flew on 10 March 1978, just a little more than two years after the order was signed. The amazing first prototype was flown by test pilot Jean Coureau at Mach 1.3 on its first flight. On 18 September 1978 the first prototype made its public debut at the Farnborough Air Show. By 11 October 1980, five prototypes had been completed, four as ordered by the French government, and one as an export demonstrator. The five also included one two-seat trainer version. On 20 November 1982, the first production Mirage 2000

Above: The Mirage 2000 cockpit. The HUD is perched atop the front instrument panel. At the pilot's left and right sides are the radar control and navigation control stations.

destined for the *Armee de l'Air* made its maiden flight. By June 1984, the first Mirage 2000 squadron was operational in the *Armee de l'Air.* On 2 February and 21 September 1983 the first and second prototypes of the Mirage 2000N long-range penetration version made their first flights. In October 1984, the air force of India was the first to receive the export version of the Mirage 2000.

THE MIRAGE 2000 IN DETAIL

The Mirage 2000 is a thoroughly modern multirole fighter designed for ser-vice both with the French *Armee de l'Air* and for export, with the latter seen by the French government as being no less important than the former. Its delta wing, swept back at 58 degrees is similar to, but 15 percent greater in area, than that of the Mirage III which the Mirage 2000 is designed to replace. Though the aircraft is composed primarily of titanium and special steels, extensive use has been made of non-metallic carbon-epoxy composite materials in the construction of such components as the tail, wing flaps and landing gear doors. There are three Mirage 2000 subtypes, the basic single-seat air defense/interceptor fighter (French designation Mirage 2000C), the two-seat training version (French designation Mirage 2000B) and the two-seat longer-range penetration fighter-bomber (French designation Mirage 2000N). The last is equipped with special avionics systems and terrain-following radar for low-level operations.

The pressurized cockpit of the Mirage is equipped with the Martin-Baker F10Q ejection seat. The flight-control system is

MIRAGE 2000

	2000B	2000C
Year first deployed:	1984	1984
Type:	Two-seat combat-capable trainer	Single-seat interceptor
Power Plant:	One SNECMA M53-5 turbofan @ 12,125 lb thrust (19,841 w/afterburner)	One SNECMA M53-5 turbofan @ 12,125 lb thrust (19,841 w/afterburner)
Wingspan:	29 ft 5 in	29 ft 5 in
Length:	47 ft 9 in	47 ft 1 in
Height:	16 ft 10.75 in	17 ft
Wing Area:	441.3 sq ft	441.3 sq ft
Gross Weight:	37,480 lb	37,480 lb
Empty Weight:	16,755 lb	16,534 lb
Maximum Speed:	Mach 2.3 @ altitude 690 mph @ sea level	Mach 2.3 @ altitude 690 mph @ sea level
Range:	920 mi normal; 2073 mi external tanks	920 mi normal; 2073 mi external tanks
Service Ceiling:	59,000 ft	59,000 ft
Fuel Capacity:	875 imp gal; 1909 gal w/external tanks	875 imp gal; 1909 gal w/external tanks
Fixed Armament:	Two DEFA 554 30mm cannons, 125 rpg	Two DEFA 554 30mm cannons, 125 rpg
Users:	Abu Dhabi, Egypt, France, Greece, India, Peru	Abu Dhabi, Egypt, France, Greece, India, Peru

a state-of-the-art fly-by-wire electronic system designed for much easier control than the earlier Mirage aircraft. The French electronics firm, Thomson–CSF, is the major avionics subcontractor, supplying such systems as the 62-mile RDM multi-mode radar (Antilope V in Mirage 2000N), the VE-130 Head-Up Display (HUD), the VHC-180 cockpit data display, Serval radar warning receiver and the ESD electronic countermeasures system with VCM-65 display. Other avionics include the Sfena 605 autopilot, the Matra Spirale passive countermeasures system and the LMT Deltac tactical air navigation (TACAN) system.

The aircraft is powered by a single M53 turbofan engine developed by the French aircraft engine builder SNECMA, under the guidance of project engineer Claude Sprung. Though originally designed for use in twin-engined aircraft, the M53 has proven to be a good match for the needs of the relatively light Mirage 2000.

Left: A French air force Mirage 2000B two-seat trainer of squadron *Cigognes* in flight.

Below: The Mirage 2000 assembly line at Dassault-Breguet Bordeaux-Merignae production facility.

Right: French fighter pilots of squadron *Cigognes*, with their warplanes, ready for inspection.

Opposite below: This underview of a Mirage 2000 shows its eight 400kg bombs, two Matra Magic missiles, two fuel drop tanks and the air refueling probe in the extended position.

Befitting the missions of a multirole aircraft, the armament capability of the Mirage 2000 is widely varied and flexible to meet any requirement. There are nine attachment points for external stores: five under the fuselage, and two under each wing. These points can accommodate a variety of weapons, electronic equipment and external fuel tanks. The weapons include various combinations of air-to-air and air-to-surface missiles, the Dassault-Breguet CC 630 twin 30mm cannon pod, anti-runway bombs, conventional gravity bombs and (in the case of the Mirage 2000N) the ASMP tactical nuclear missile. Other stores include camera pods, electronic countermeasures pods, fuel tanks and the Intertechnique 231-300 inflight refueling pod which permits the Mirage 2000 to function as an aerial refueling tanker, helping to top off the fuel tanks of companion aircraft in emergencies.

THE MIRAGE 2000 IN SERVICE

In accordance with its plans to make the Mirage 2000 its first-line fighter for the 1980s and early 1990s, the French *Armee de l'Air* accepted its first operational aircraft in 1983. On 2 July 1984 fighter squadron *Cigognes* at Dijon became the first operational unit with 10 Mirage 2000Cs and 4 Mirage 2000Bs. Fighter squadron *Alsace* followed in 1985, with tactical fighter squadron *Côte d'Or* scheduled for 1987. The first Mirage 2000N nuclear strike aircraft joined squadron 4 at Luxevil in 1986 and were followed by squadron 7 at Saint-Dizier. By 1988, 36 Mirage 2000Ns are scheduled to be in service with five squadrons.

The first foreign contracts for the Mirage 2000 came with Egypt's January 1982 order for 20 of the aircraft, which included four trainers to be delivered under the designation Mirage 2000BM. India ordered 40 aircraft in October 1982, with the first deliveries coming exactly two years later. Four of the Indian aircraft will be two-seat trainers delivered under the designation Mirage 2000TH. These two initial orders were followed by sales to Peru in December 1982, Abu Dhabi in May 1983 and Greece in March 1985. Peru ordered 26 aircraft and Abu Dhabi 18, while Greece bought 40 and took an option on 20 more.

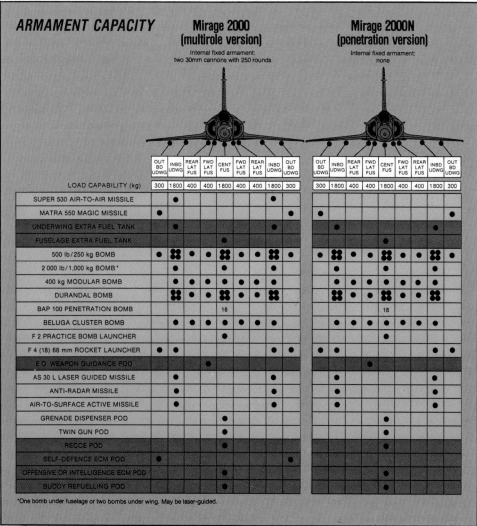

ARMAMENT CAPACITY

Mirage 2000 (multirole version) — Internal fixed armament: two 30mm cannons with 250 rounds

Mirage 2000N (penetration version) — Internal fixed armament: none

	OUT BD UDWG	INBD UDWG	REAR LAT FUS	FWD LAT FUS	CENT FUS	FWD LAT FUS	REAR LAT FUS	INBD UDWG	OUT BD UDWG	OUT BD UDWG	INBD UDWG	REAR LAT FUS	FWD LAT FUS	CENT FUS	FWD LAT FUS	REAR LAT FUS	INBD UDWG	OUT BD UDWG
LOAD CAPABILITY (kg)	300	1800	400	400	1800	400	400	1800	300	300	1800	400	400	1800	400	400	1800	300
SUPER 530 AIR-TO-AIR MISSILE		●						●										
MATRA 550 MAGIC MISSILE	●								●	●								●
UNDERWING EXTRA FUEL TANK		●						●			●						●	
FUSELAGE EXTRA FUEL TANK					●									●				
500 lb/250 kg BOMB	●	●●	●	●	●●	●	●	●●	●	●	●●		●	●●	●		●●	●
2 000 lb/1,000 kg BOMB*		●			●			●			●			●			●	
400 kg MODULAR BOMB		●	●		●		●	●			●	●	●	●	●	●	●	
DURANDAL BOMB		●●	●	●	●●	●	●	●●			●●	●	●	●●	●	●	●●	
BAP 100 PENETRATION BOMB					18									18				
BELUGA CLUSTER BOMB		●	●	●	●	●	●	●			●	●	●	●	●	●	●	
F 2 PRACTICE BOMB LAUNCHER					●									●				
F 4 (18) 68 mm ROCKET LAUNCHER	●	●						●	●	●	●						●	●
E O WEAPON GUIDANCE POD				●									●					
AS 30 L LASER GUIDED MISSILE		●						●			●						●	
ANTI-RADAR MISSILE		●						●			●						●	
AIR-TO-SURFACE ACTIVE MISSILE		●						●			●						●	
GRENADE DISPENSER POD					●									●				
TWIN GUN POD					●									●				
RECCE POD					●									●				
SELF-DEFENCE ECM POD	●								●	●								●
OFFENSIVE OR INTELLIGENCE ECM POD					●									●				
BUDDY REFUELLING POD					●									●				

*One bomb under fuselage or two bombs under wing. May be laser-guided.

ROCKWELL
B-1

A LONG WAIT

The original idea for the B-1 is traceable to the Advanced Manned Strategic Aircraft (AMSA) project begun in 1962, but really goes back to the mid-1950s when the Boeing B-52 Stratofortress was becoming the backbone of the US Air Force's Strategic Air Command (SAC). It is customary when dealing with combat aircraft to fight obsolescence by beginning work on a plane's successor as soon as the former goes into service. When the B-52 joined SAC in 1955, engineering work had already begun toward a number of aircraft, one of which would *certainly* replace it by the end of the 1960s. It is probably the highest tribute that can be paid the B-52 to note that it outlived its intended successors, and will soldier on into the 1990s.

Both the B-58 and the B-70 had been rejected as B-52 replacements by the time that the USAF's AMSA requirement was finally published in 1965, calling for the new bomber to be operational by 1980. Under the Defense Department nomenclature reorganization, all combat aircraft numbering was restarted at one. The new AMSA bomber was, of course, designated B-1. It is an interesting point of trivia that in the twenty years preceding 1962,

40 bomber projects received 'B' designations (including 19 that actually went into service), while in the same length of time since 1962 there was only one, the B-1.

The Air Force entertained proposals from several aircraft manufacturers, finally settling on the Los Angeles Division of North American Rockwell (now the North American Aircraft Operations Division of Rockwell International), the same firm that had built the wartime B-25 and the huge Mach 3 B-70. A contract was issued on 6 June 1970, calling for five flight-test aircraft and two non-flying airframes to be used in structural tests. General Electric, the engine contractor, was asked to build 40 F101 turbofan engines, which translated as one complete replacement set for each of the five prototypes. This initial order was reduced in January 1971 to three flight-test aircraft, one non-flying airframe, and 27 engines. At the same time, the constantly evolving design for the new plane was frozen and production began.

The actual assembly of the first of what was intended to be 250 B-1s began at the Air Force's Plant 42 at Palmdale, California on 15 March 1972. This aircraft rolled out on 26 October 1974 and made its maiden flight on 23 December. The second B-1 prototype (the avionics systems

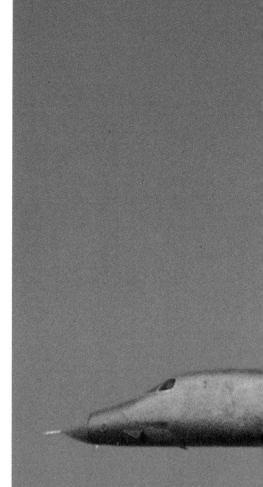

Left: US Air Force Lt Col Leroy Schroeder of the B-1A bomber aircraft test team looks out the left cockpit window of the warplane as it taxis on the runway. The B-1A, in desert camouflage, had just completed a fly-by and landing at Andrews AFB near Washington, DC following the 1982 Farnborough Air Show.

Above: The first Rockwell B-1B bomber of the US Air Force Strategic Air Command. The manned bomber has long been the foundation of the American triad nuclear deterrent defense strategy and is considered by many to be its most reliable retaliatory weapon. The other two legs of the triad are US Air Force silo-based Intercontinental Ballistic Missiles and US Navy Submarine-Launched Ballistic Missiles.

Top right: Next to the top-view silhouette of the B-1 is the military insignia of the United States, Rockwell's only customer for this awesome strategic warplane.

Below: This cutaway view of a B-1A reveals Boeing Short Range Attack Missiles (SRAM) on rotary launchers in forward and aft bays. The middle bay is empty and the rotary launcher can be seen in detail. The improved B-1B would have a movable bulkhead wall between forward weapons bays *(see illustration, page 108).* The B-1A cockpit here had an escape capsule, rather than the ejection seats that would come in the B-1B.

ROCKWELL B-1

	B-1A	B-1B
Year first deployed:	1974	1985
Type:	Variable-geometry strategic bomber	Variable-geometry strategic bomber
Power Plant:	Four General Electric F-101-GE-100 turbofans @ 30,000 lb thrust each	Four General Electric F-101-GE-102 turbofans @ 30,000 lb thrust each
Wingspan:	136 ft 8.5 in spread 75 ft 2.5 in swept	136 ft 8.5 in spread; 78 ft 2.5 in swept
Length:	150 ft 2.5 in	147 ft
Gross Weight:	389,000 lb	477,000 lb
Maximum Speed:	Mach 2.1 @ altitude	Mach 1 @ altitude
Range:	6100 mi normal	6200 mi +
Service Ceiling:	50,000 ft	50,000 ft
Fixed Armament:	None	None
Users:	USAF	USAF

test aircraft) did not fly until 14 June 1976, three months after the first flight of the third prototype on 26 March.

Jimmy Carter replaced Republican Gerald Ford in the White House in January 1977. Carter had campaigned for the presidency on a platform of reducing defense spending, particularly spending on strategic weapons, and the B-1 program was a prime target. When he moved into the Oval Office, the new President inherited two production contracts that had been issued in December 1976, for two groups of B-1s, totaling 11 aircraft. Nevertheless, he made good on his campaign promises and canceled the B-1 production program on 30 June 1977. The initial test phase, along with completion of a fourth prototype, was allowed to continue, however.

Over the next 46 months, until the prescribed end of the B-1 test phase, the first three prototypes made 79, 60 and 138 test

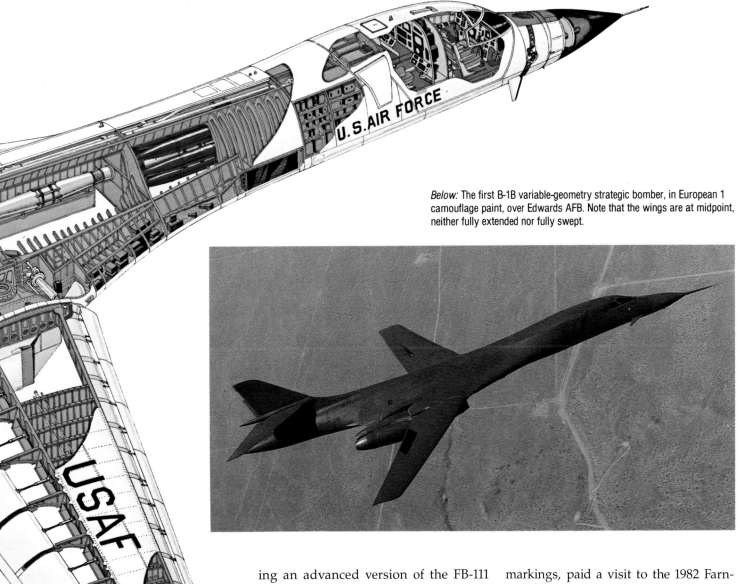

Below: The first B-1B variable-geometry strategic bomber, in European 1 camouflage paint, over Edwards AFB. Note that the wings are at midpoint, neither fully extended nor fully swept.

flights respectively, totaling 1516 hours of flying time. During this period, the second prototype achieved a top speed of Mach 2.22 on 5 October 1978. The fourth prototype, which joined the program on 14 February 1979, logged 378 hours during 70 flights before the program ended in April 1981.

By this time, the Carter administration had been replaced by the more defense-conscious administration of Ronald Reagan, who was willing to address the need for a replacement for the aging B-52 fleet. Several options were studied under the Long Range Combat Aircraft (LRCA) evaluation program, including develop-ing an advanced version of the FB-111 strategic fighter-bomber, and waiting 10 years for the arrival for the Northrop B-2 Advanced Technology Bomber (ATB, or 'Stealth'). In the end, the best choice seemed to be a strategic bomber that was *already* under development.

On 2 October 1981 President Reagan officially asked Rockwell to develop a new version of the B-1 which would retain the original's general appearance, while incorporating the state-of-the-art avionics and 'Stealth' technology that had evolved during the 10 years since the original B-1 design had been frozen. The new aircraft would be designated B-1B, while the original four B-1 aircraft were redesignated B-1A.

Since it would take Rockwell three years to rebuild the assembly line and construct a new airframe from the ground up, the first step in B-1B development would be the modification of the second and fourth B-1As to B-1B standard. This would allow the avionics systems of the B-1B to be tested several years before the first new airframe was ready.

The number four B-1A prototype, painted in three-tone desert camouflage markings, paid a visit to the 1982 Farn-borough Air Show in England, where it was the star attraction. The white number two B-1A prototype joined the 'B-1B' test program in March 1983, with a huge B-1B painted on its tail in red, white and blue. The third prototype was put in long-term storage, while the first was earmarked to be cannibalized for spare parts. The second prototype, the plane that had been flown at Mach 2.22 five years earlier, logged 261 hours in 66 flights in the B-1B test program over the next 17 months.

THE B-1B IN DETAIL

The three years of B-1B development, both on the factory floor and in the two converted B-1A test beds, had yielded a much refined aircraft. The avionics were a decade newer, the bomb load greater, and the radar signature vastly smaller. Though the B-1B was the same size as the B-1A, its image on radar was one-tenth the size, thanks to redesigned engine nacelles and radar-absorbing composites.

The fuselage is nearly 150 feet long and built of aluminum, titanium and non-metallic composite components. The tail

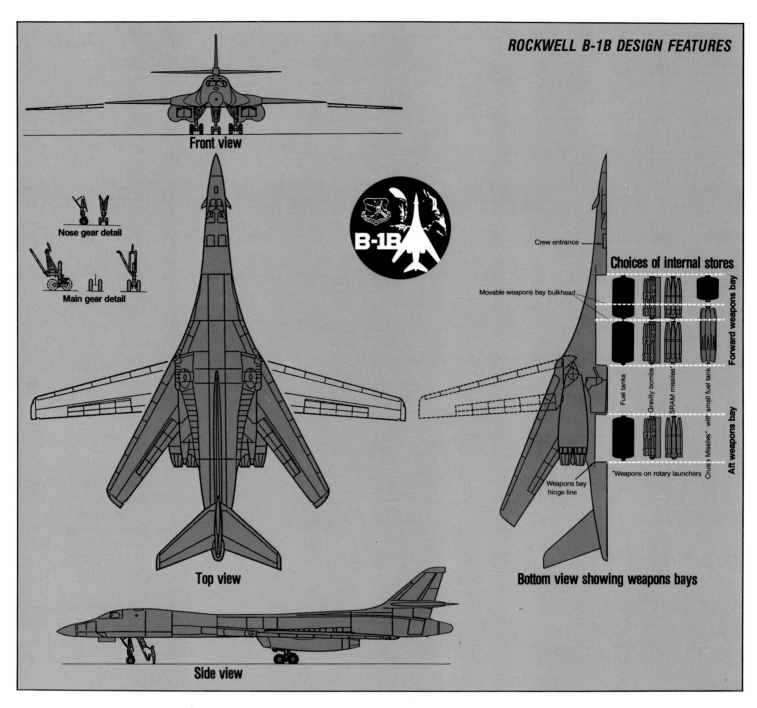

Front view

Nose gear detail

Main gear detail

Top view

Side view

Crew entrance

Choices of internal stores

Movable weapons bay bulkhead

Forward weapons bay

Fuel tanks

Gravity bombs

SRAM missiles

Aft weapons bay

Cruise Missiles* with small fuel tank

Weapons bay hinge line

*Weapons on rotary launchers

Bottom view showing weapons bays

unit is made of titanium and aluminum alloy components, with movable surfaces driven hydraulically with fly-by-wire backup. The wings are of the variable-geometry or 'swing wing' type. They can be swept back to 67 degrees and forward to 15 degrees, using four hydraulic motors that can be operated by only two of the plane's four hydraulic systems. A torque shaft connects them and keeps the two wings symmetrical. The wings are constructed primarily of aluminum and contain fuel tanks.

The engines are housed in specially designed nacelles located under the aft part of the wing root. The four General Electric F101 turbofans each deliver 30,000 pounds of thrust, compared with 17,000 pounds of thrust from the Pratt & Whitney turbofans of the B-52H. Where the B-1A was designed for (and tested at)

speeds in excess of Mach 2, the B-1B is designed for what the Air Force calls 'high subsonic' (Mach .9) speeds at lower altitudes, although it has a Mach 1.2 capability. The range of the B-1B is greater than that of either the B-52 or B-1A, making it less dependent on aerial refueling. With aerial refueling, however, the B-1B can fly to any place in the world and back without having to stop for fuel.

Within the framework of the airframe and pushed by the power of the engines, the 'heart' and 'mind' of the B-1B are its avionics systems, both vastly improved over those of the B-1A. The Eaton AN/ALQ-161 defensive avionics (electronic countermeasures, ECM) system was developed to support and protect the aircraft while it operates deep in the heart of hostile airspace.

Despite its sophistication—or perhaps *because* of it—the AN/ALQ-161 proved to be the B-1B's Achilles heel. Even as late as August 1988, a House Armed Services Committee investigation revealed that the system was able to accomplish only half of its intended mission, leaving the B-1B potentially vulnerable and aircrews probably yearning for the days when bombers were protected by a tail-mounted cannon.

It was suggested that the B-1B might be retrofitted with the ITT Avionics AN/ALQ-172, which was then in use aboard SAC's B-52 fleet, and which had 180 degrees of coverage, versus 120 degrees for the troubled AN/ALQ-161. Although the AN/ALQ-172 system was perceived as being more reliable, the cost of re-wiring and reconfiguring the system installation was seen as a reason to

Above: This B-1B, *Star of Abilene*, is assigned to the 96th Bomb Wing based at Dyess AFB near Abilene, Texas.

continue with efforts to improve the AN/ALQ-161 system.

The offensive avionics include a high energy inertial navigation system, a Doppler velocity sensor, a radar altimeter, countermeasures displays and an Offensive Radar System (ORS). The ORS includes a low-observable, phased-array antenna, and provides low-altitude, terrain-following and precise navigational functions.

The offensive weapons are carried in three internal bays and can also be carried on external weapons pylons. The two forward weapons bays are actually a 31 foot, three inch double bay with a movable bulkhead, which permits accommodation of the 20 foot, nine inch Boeing AGM-86 Air Launched Cruise Missile (ALCM), a weapon which the B-1A could not carry. In addition to eight ALCMs, which can be mounted on a rotary launcher in the forward weapons bay, the B-1B can carry eight Short Range Attack Missiles (SRAM) in the aft bay. By removing the ALCMs and centering the partition in the forward double bay, a total of 24 SRAMs can be carried. The B-1B could also carry up to 24 nuclear bombs. For missions requiring conventional ordnance, high explosive bombs can be carried internally. Fuel tanks can also be carried internally, and weapons (including 12 ALCMs or SRAMs) can be carried on eight external pylon attachments located below the fuselage, adjacent to the big bomber's weapons bay doors.

THE B-1B IN SERVICE

The first flight of a production B-1B took place on 18 October 1984, six weeks after its rollout, and five months ahead of schedule. On 31 October, after initial inflight tests of the new aircraft's systems, it was flown the short distance from Palmdale to Edwards AFB, completing 4.8 hours of flying time. A third flight of 5.5 hours on 14 November completed the initial test program.

By June 1985, the second production B-1B had been completed and had undergone six weeks of flight tests and was ready for delivery to the Strategic Air Command's 96th Bomb Wing at Dyess AFB, Texas. A year later, 15 aircraft had been delivered to the Air Force. After having delivered only four aircraft during 1985, Rockwell reached a point in December 1986 after which it would produce no fewer than four a *month*. Meanwhile, the 4018th Combat Crew Training Squadron at Dyess was turning out the crews to man the big planes.

On 14 April 1987 a Dyess-based B-1B took off on a 21 hour, 40 minute nonstop demonstration of the bomber's endurance capability. Taking off at a gross weight of 413,000 pounds — 73,000 pounds above normal for operational training missions — the aircraft covered 9411 miles on a course that took it across Alaska to within 160 nautical miles of the Soviet Union.

Dyess AFB had reached IOC (Initial Operating Capability) with 15 aircraft in September 1986 and had its full complement of B-1Bs by December. Having received its first bomber in January 1987, Ellsworth AFB received its 35th, and last, in September. Grand Forks AFB, North Dakota, received its 17th, and last, B-1B in December as deliveries began to McConnell AFB, Kansas.

The 100th and final B-1B was officially delivered to SAC on 30 April 1988, two months ahead of schedule. This B-1B was also the 17th, and final, of the complement of aircraft assigned to the 384th Bomb Wing at McConnell AFB, Kansas.

With one B-1B having been lost in a crash on 28 September 1987 during a low-level training mission near La Junta, Colorado, the total fleet consisted of 99 aircraft at the time of the final delivery. Two more were lost in November 1988, bringing the total to 97. Three of this total (including the first B-1B) were assigned to Edwards AFB for test and evaluation, and the remainder were assigned to SAC for operations and training at McConnell AFB, Ellsworth AFB, Grand Forks AFB and Dyess AFB.

As part of SAC's overall modernization program, the B-1B, along with the Northrop B-2 'Stealth' bomber (see following pages), will give the Strategic Air Command its most effective force since the days of Curtis LeMay in the 1950s. If the B-52's record is any indication, much of the B-1B fleet will still be in service in 2015.

NORTHROP
B-2 STEALTH

THE MYSTERY SHIP

She spent the decade of the 1980s lurking in her secret lair. She was like a mythical beast, well known, but never seen — the stuff of legends. An airplane that was invisible on radar. She was ethereal and magic.

From the time she was first mentioned in public during the 1980 presidential campaign, she had a mystique that went far beyond any facts that we knew about her. If it hadn't been for the fact that President Jimmy Carter desperately needed a weapons system to hang his hat on, she might have remained secret for another decade.

Carter had come to office in 1976, during an era when— because of the Vietnam War—the American electorate was sick of everything military. He had promised to cancel the Rockwell B-1 program and he did. By 1980, times had changed. The United States was beginning to pay the price for years of neglecting its defense establishment. Carter was running an uphill election battle against Ronald Reagan, who promised to rebuild America's once-proud military might.

Jimmy Carter had an ace in the hole, however. He knew that the Air Force was secretly developing a revolutionary type of strategic bomber that employed a basket of technologies known as 'stealth' that would make it virtually invisible to enemy radar. In August 1988 he decided to let Defense Secretary Harold Brown leak just enough information about this 'stealth bomber' to make him appear to the public as one who quietly and secretly 'cared' about defense. Carter's ploy failed to get him elected, but it gave aviation enthusiasts and Soviet spies their first tantalizing inkling of the aircraft that would be 'the mystery plane of the decade.'

The Reagan Administration brought down the veil of secrecy upon the 'stealth bomber' project, and little more was known for years. By 1985 it was learned that the prime contractor for the mystery ship was Northrop, and this in turn led to

speculation that the new airplane would have a 'flying wing' configuration, because Northrop's only other heavy bombers had been the YB-35 and YB-49 Flying Wings of the early 1950s. It was also learned that when President Reagan revived the B-1 program, there was a behind closed doors debate over whether to try to bring 'stealth' on line sooner to obviate the need for the B-1. Nevertheless, the 'stealth bomber' remained a mystery, referred to by the US Air Force simply as the Advanced Technology Bomber (ATB).

In 1987 plastic model kits of the Northrop ATB appeared, but they were based only on guesswork, because nobody really knew what the new aircraft would look like. An educated guess supposed — correctly—that the ATB would receive the B-2 service designation. It was an obvious supposition but, again, until 1988 nobody really knew—except those sworn to secrecy. It was revealed later that a major redesign took place in 1984 which would ultimately result in the first flight being pushed back from 1987 to 1989. The redesign was a product of the fact that the ATB was so profoundly unique.

In September 1987 this writer visited the Air Force's Plant 42 complex at Palmdale, California and was shown the 'factory where the airplane that doesn't exist

Above: Northrop's remarkable YB-49 Flying Wing on an early flight over the Mojave Desert in 1949, not far from Palmdale, where three B-2s are seen *(right)* during assembly in 1989.

is being built.' A look behind the doors was not included, but it was clear from the shape of the hangar behind those doors that the 'flying wing' prediction was correct. It was also clear that the Air Force was taking security very seriously. The B-2 facility, which was located across the runway from where Rockwell was wrapping up production of the B-1, was surrounded by 30-foot trenches, 20-foot fences and the biggest dogs anyone in Palmdale could remember seeing.

And so it remained. The announcement of an impending rollout came and went in the autumn of 1987 and reappeared the following summer. By now another presidential election campaign was in progress, so the Air Force made the decision to postpone the rollout until 22 November 1988, two weeks after the election.

When it finally did come, the B-2 rollout was the most heavily restricted *public* rollout in history. Indeed, there was a public rollout only because the Air Force decided that it would be impossible to flight test so large an aircraft in total secrecy. Only 500 guests were on hand,

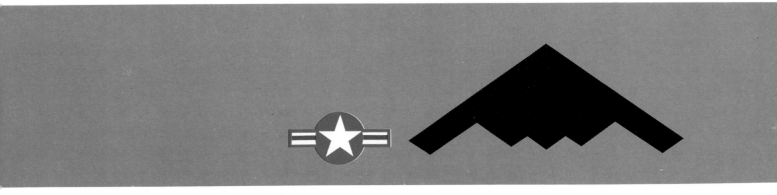

and armed guards with German Shepherds outnumbered reporters by a ratio of four to one. A specially prepared orchestral work, the *Stealth Fanfare*, was played by an Air Force band. Nobody was allowed to look behind the B-2, but an *Aviation Week* photographer managed to take several photos of its top from above restricted air space.

The initial flight of the strange new airplane was set first for January 1989, postponed to Easter, and in March it was pushed back to summer. It was in March 1989 that a proposal was made to do minimum flight readiness preparations at Palmdale and then fly the first YB-2 prototype 20 miles 'over the fence' to nearby Edwards AFB, thus symbolically 'delivering' it to the Air Force.

Prior to the rollout, the Air Force had already announced its intention to spend a further $36.6 billion on the program, which would include a total of 132 B-2 bombers, along with support facilities and spares. Most of these would be earmarked for operational duty with the Strategic Air Command (SAC), with three or four serving with the Air Force Systems Command (AFSC) as test beds for ongoing systems upgrade projects. The first base to become operational with a B-2 wing was to be Whiteman AFB near Kansas City, which was expected to receive its first bird in fiscal year 1991, and where 34 covered aircraft alert shelters were being built.

Northrop and the Air Force chose 10 July 1989 to initiate the B-2's taxi tests, and

the first flight began at 6:37 am on 17 July with Northrop B-2 chief test pilot Bruce Hinds and Air Force Colonel Richard Couch in the cockpit. Much to the chagrin of critics, the flight went smoothly and the big bat touched down lightly at Edwards AFB at 8:29 am. Two further flights by the first prototype were made within a month, as the second and third B-2s neared completion in the big Palmdale hangar.

However, when the Bush administration announced that the annual procurement cost for the B-2 would be $8 billion, Congressional Armed Services Committee Chairman Les Aspin moaned that 'There are only 12 countries in the world that have defense budgets greater than $8 billion a year. We would be spending more on the B-2 than any Warsaw Pact country spends except Russia and East Germany. Is it conceivable that we are going to do this? No chance!'

Prior to the B-2's first flight, it was widely reported that the unit cost of the B-2 would be $532 million, a figure arrived at by dividing the $70.2 billion program cost by 132 aircraft. However, Northrop pointed out that the total included $22.5 billion that had already been spent on development, and that additional aircraft would cost less than half what was being bantered about in the press. By eliminating training and base construction from the program, the actual unit cost was in the area of $250 million.

Armed with this information, supporters of the B-2 in both the House of Representatives and the Senate headed off attempts to kill the B-2 program entirely, but they did accept delays in procurement that would save money in the near term, but which would, ironically, force the ultimate cost higher by spreading out the time it would take to build 132 B-2s.

THE B-2 IN DETAIL

The aircraft that was first seen in public on 22 November 1988 was unlike anything that had been seen in public since the days of Northrop's other great 'flying wings' nearly 40 years before. A futuristic, batlike creature, the B-2 differed from the YB-35 and YB-49 in that it has no vertical tail surfaces. Extremely sophisticated, quadruple-redundant, fly-by-wire digital electronic controls had eliminated the need for conventional rudders, as well as serving to solve the stability problem that was the Achilles heel of the YB-35 and YB-49. Primary flight control consisted of three elevon surfaces on each wing and a rudder/spoiler at each wingtip. The outboard trailing edge had the drag rudder

and the next inboard trailing edge surface had two more elevons. This system ingeniously eliminated the need for vertical tail surfaces and made it possible for the B-2 to make turns without a thrust-vectoring system, which some analysts had predicted that the long secret ship would use.

Three-dimensional Northrop Computer Aided Design (NCAD) systems played an important role in the development and manufacturing process, providing manufacturing accuracy and engineering complex surface tolerances, helping engineers to blend and shape the aircraft to achieve its low observable characteristics. It has been said that these systems, which are as advanced as the B-2 itself, saved a great deal in terms of both time and money, but there is really no way of knowing, because both NCAD and B-2

are so revolutionary that there is nothing with which to compare them!

It is known that the 3D nature of NCAD resulted in a much streamlined machining and metal cutting process because precise measurements and 3D digital imagery eliminated the industry standard that necessitated up to seven preliminary cuttings, using wood or foam core, before the final adjustment of the tooling dies was possible. An industry standard of 20 to 40 percent waste in the process of cutting precision lengths of titanium tubing was cut to three percent because of NCAD.

The B-2 is a huge airplane, with a wingspan greater than that of the B-1B, and almost as great as the B-52's. Its precise weapons-carrying capability is unknown, but it is probably no greater than the B-1B's, and like the B-1B, the

NORTHROP B-2

Year first deployed:	1989
Type:	Low observable strategic bomber
Power Plant:	Four General Electric F118-GE-100 turbofans @ 19,000 lb thrust each
Wingspan:	172 ft
Length:	69 ft
Height:	17 ft
Maximum Range:	5000 mi without refueling
Service Ceiling:	50,000 ft
User:	US Air Force

entire payload is carried in an internal bomb bay, which contains a rotary launcher capable of being configured with Air Launched Cruise Missiles (ALCM), Short Range Attack Missiles (SRAM) or a choice of conventional or nuclear bombs.

The B-2 is aerial-refuelable, thus extending its range to 'intercontinental' and making it the equal of the B-52 or B-1B. In terms of crew size, however, the B-2 is significantly different. Whereas it takes four men to operate the B-1B, advanced cockpit automation makes it possible for the B-2 to be flown on operational missions by a crew of just two, although provisions exist for carrying a third crew member, or observer.

While Northrop is the primary contractor for the B-2 program, both LTV Aerospace and the Boeing Military Airplane

Above: The 1988 rollout of the B-2 was accompanied by strains of the *Stealth Fanfare*, while the first flight *(facing page)* on 17 July 1989, which ended with a perfect touchdown at Edwards AFB *(below)*, was accompanied by the strained cries of congressional budget cutters.

Company are known to be high profile subcontractors. Boeing is significant by its presence in the program because of its pre-eminent role in building the Air Force's most important strategic bombers, from the B-17 in 1935 to the B-52, which was last in production in 1963 and which will be in service until beyond 1999. It was reported that Boeing actually sought to be elevated to prime contractor status during a behind-the-scenes program crisis in the mid-1980s. The Boeing presence was immediately noticeable on rollout day to those who recognized the 757/767 jetliner landing gear upon which the B-2 rested.

When everything is said and done,

however, the most unique and important feature of the B-2—indeed its entire purpose for being—is its stealth technology. Stealth is, in fact, a whole basket of technologies designed to make the airplane virtually invisible to radar. These include contours and surfaces that absorb, rather than reflect, radar waves, thus giving the B-2 the radar signature more characteristic of a bird than a B-52.

As Secretary of the Air Force Edward Aldridge said on 22 November 1988, the B-2's stealth characteristics render Soviet radar 'ineffective, because the type of air defense systems they have will not be able to detect this aircraft except at very short ranges. The whole idea behind this aircraft is to hold targets at risk in the Soviet Union. That's what deterrence is all about... making sure the war doesn't start in the first place!'

INDEX